ADVANCE PRAISE FOR *THE DIGITAL INFERNO*:

'This book is visionary and practical and both are needed at this time as the digital inferno spreads, setting fire to more and more elements of daily life.' – Tom Bourner, Emeritus Professor of Personal and Professional Development, University of Brighton, co-author of *Workshops That Work*

'An exciting book, full of hope for the future. By applying the concept of mindfulness to digital interactions, Paul Levy shows how we can get the most out of technology without losing touch with our essential humanity. Great stuff – thoughtful, insightful and very timely.' – Sue Palmer, author of *Toxic Childhood*

'An insightful guide for those seeking to consciously navigate the noise and confusion of the digital age.' – Daniel T. Jones, author of *The Machine That Changed The World* and founder of the Lean Enterprise Academy

'A fascinating and thought-provoking survey of our digital times.' – Cliff McNish, author of *The Doomspell Trilogy*

'Our generation is gradually noticing the subtle effects of digital media in our lives. There are no clear answers as the effects are generative and emergent but it is useful to be mindful of the path we are creating. Paul Levy's book is an eye opener. It is written with precision and full of insights on this ongoing interplay between people and technology. It is a great book for anyone keen to regain control of their relationship with gadgets and digital media in general.' – Professor John Baptista, Associate Professor of Information Systems, University of Warwick

'A fascinating, moving and practical dance of content exploring what awfully is *and what* awe fully might be *as human civilization embraces digital virtuality. Brilliantly conceived and written.'* – Angus Jenkinson, author of *From Stress to Serenity*, Chief Organising Officer of the Civil Society Forum

DIGITAL INFERNO

USING TECHNOLOGY CONSCIOUSLY
IN YOUR LIFE AND WORK

101 WAYS TO SURVIVE AND THRIVE
IN A HYPERCONNECTED WORLD

PAUL LEVY

CLAIRVIEW

Published in Great Britain in 2014 by:
Clairview Books,
Russet, Sandy Lane,
West Hoathly,
W. Sussex RH18 5ES

E-mail: office@clairviewbooks.com

www.clairviewbooks.com

A catalogue record for this book is available from the British Library

Print book ISBN 978 1 905570 74 4
Ebook ISBN 978 1 905570 65 2

Cover by Morgan Creative featuring an image © Sergey Nivens
Typeset by DP Photosetting, Neath, West Glamorgan
Printed and bound by Gutenberg Press Ltd., Malta

To Sylvia, Cyril, Didi, Roo, Catty and Honey

Contents

Acknowledgements

I'd like to express thanks to Sevak Gulbekian and Peter Stephenson for their priceless guidance and editorial genius in helping this book to emerge out of the digital realm, into the form of a manuscript and finally a book. Thanks to the creative souls at Pavilion Gardens Café, to David Knowles, Tom Bourner, Michael Parker and Ian Powell for their listening, and their willingness not to collude. Thanks to Graham Precey for breakfasts without purpose. Thanks to Demelza Craze and Sylvia Levy for having the patience to read and re-read. And thanks to Ian Postre, an inspirer of this journey.

Introduction

It would be easy to write a book warning of the dangers of mobile technology. It would condemn the negative effects on the well-being and health of people and communities. There is, in fact, a case for condemning the addictive nature of the internet and there are hundreds of studies of the negative effects of the digital realm. If I were on a mission to have it all switched off, then I would present a one-sided case. I am not going to do that. The digital world is here. Its waves are running through your living room and through your head. It is in your pocket, it's everywhere. However, I believe we are here to meet it and my starting point is that we should meet it with self-awareness, hold our own in the face of it and not give ourselves over to it. This is what I mean by *staying awake* in the digital realm, which is what this book is mostly about.

I'm 47 years old, and here are my digital credentials. I was Head of Interaction at the Digital Workplace Group and the Intranet Benchmarking Forum for six years. I've been a senior researcher at the Centre for Research in Innovation Management at the University of Brighton for over 20 years. I have a leading edge smart phone, three tablets and four laptop computers. I also have a paper notebook in my bag and a nice pen. I'm a trained social scientist and my interests include communication, spirituality, theatre, creativity and personal development. I am an open-minded sceptic. I have over 10,000 *Twitter* followers, 900 friends on *Facebook*, and over 1000 contacts on *LinkedIn*. My blog was visited over 30,000 times last year and my various websites garnered over 150,000 unique visitors. I've made films, worked with animators and developed new ways of holding virtual conference meetings. This book is a harvest of some of that experience.

The short history of the digital realm has been one of constant flux and powerful forces blowing in from who knows where. It brings with it a shift in consciousness and new possibilities, as all new frontiers do. Is it a stepping stone towards creating heaven on earth? Is it a realm in which dreams will soon become reality? That is up to us. One thing is certain, it is flaring upwards and outwards like an inferno. I'm excited and inspired by it, and scared and fascinated by it. Whatever we think or feel about it, we must meet it if we are to shape it to our ends. To only demonize it, as some do, would be to ignore its already firm embrace.

This book will be more or less meaningful depending on how you want to relate to the digital realm. If we were all together in a room, each person might show his or her attitude to it by standing somewhere along a line. One end of this line would represent having nothing to do with the digital realm; a person standing there will think that it is anti-human and that it seduces people into fake experience and addiction. The other end of the line would represent diving blindly into digital experience. Between those extremes is the more complex position of welcoming a new technology while being armed with an understanding of its challenges and limitations.

That middle position seems the hardest to sustain because the digital realm, given the way it is designed and marketed, offers a better experience if you are *always on*. Constant system updates and feedback, automated as well as human, demand that you do something to stay in touch and on top of it. I've not met that many people in the last 20 years who are able to sustain the middle position. A person at the middle often slides towards becoming hooked. He, or she, might begin a digital session intending to have just a couple of shots only to stagger out, stupefied, after spending hours having just one more for the road, aimlessly following one more link. I call this *digital drift*. It is going to become a widely known phenomenon in the future.

Some warn of the dangers of the digital inferno and, equally, it has its strong defenders.

Our privacy is under threat! – No, that's a myth; we have more control than ever.

The batteries and the electricity required to run laptops and underground servers leave a big carbon footprint. – No, this is a new way to communicate without the even heavier carbon footprint of flying and driving to see each other.

Computer games are de-sensitizing our children to violence. – No, there's no evidence to support that; rather, tablet computers running collaborative software for four-year-olds are nurturing values of community and cooperation.

Our children are becoming lazy, forgetting how to add and multiply. – No! The web is a place for active exploration and problem solving. It develops our thinking.

Our bodies are becoming sick through lack of exercise and healthy movement. – But we'll soon be cyborgs, with enhanced capability and robots will serve our every need. Anyway, buy a decent chair!

We are isolated from each other by it. – No, we are more connected than ever.

To adherents of digital living and working, any criticism is 'uncool', a spoiling tactic, a sign of being out of touch. *It is the greatest invention, the most awesome, planet-changing phenomenon humanity has ever produced, so why knock it?*

The arguments and statistics for and against are bamboozling and contradictory. And our relation to the digital realm is contradictory. We celebrate the arrival of a new smartphone ('got it free on the same tariff!') while bemoaning our loss of privacy and ritually loving to hate *Facebook*. But it remains true that, whatever charges we bring, these gadgets help to create an unprecedented single planet family. It is exciting and it is also frightening. Both together. There will be neither simple indictment nor unqualified endorsement. The message here is about how we find in ourselves the right relation to an inferno – a swirling, hot storm of change, confusion, addiction, passion, possibility, lockdown, manipulation, creativity, cliché, fakery and brutal honesty. It's all in there. It is developing faster than our ability to understand it. Behind it stand powerful and often unseen forces of commercial interest and change. Some technical visionaries see the digital world becoming a kind of 'hive mind' and we, the masses, will be the drones, lost in it and ruled by it. Being really *in* it can redefine people and determine many hours of their lives. Just to enter it is to become subject to its underlying 'rules' and to adopt some of its behavioural patterns. It can become the focus of your attention and disconnect you from the physical world. It offers contentment at a price.

This book contains stories, advice and practical ways to adapt in a healthy way to a giant development in our lifetime which has reached into every corner of life in an incredibly short space of time – and has become part of our social body before we have digested it. I will often present a dark view of the digital realm and point to its potential to do harm but – and this is the point – we will meet this challenge better if we do so while being as wide awake as possible.

Even while working on this book I felt myself drifting towards doing other things rather than completing it. This is because of a tiredness that began to creep over me the moment I began to use my first mobile phone. Actually, it must have been earlier, when I was couch-surfing daytime television at ten in the morning when the sun was shining outside. The tiredness is only forgotten when I spend time away from my various devices *or if I use them but in a very specific way.* I hope to describe this way in this book. It is a way of stepping back from constant digital activity, getting some distance from it and paying more attention to the *live* version of the real world.

Perhaps this comes across as being down on the digital realm. That is not the intention. This book is not an attack on the digital realm. For over 20 years I have dived into it as a blogger, a member of chat rooms, a barefoot poet in *Second Life*, an online conference facilitator, a host of an internet radio show and as a speaker at virtual meetings. I've observed, reflected and connected with leading thinkers and practitioners in the field. I've met some who are immersed in it to the extent of being passive and addicted. They spend hours in there which to them feel wasted and lost forever. Some are worried for themselves, or for their kids.

I've met others who engage with it in disciplined ways and are under no illusions about its darker side. These are members of a growing community of people who seek to avoid losing themselves in it and becoming pawns of its underlying commercial game plans. What they seek is a more conscious way through it in order to derive the benefits and manage the dangers.

It is quite possible to go right in, and seem to become cleverer while definitely becoming colder. This is what I found when I became fully immersed in it as a researcher who was trying to understand it. This book will expose this cold realm of quantity, and assert that quality, nuance and subtlety are vital for human beings. However complex quantity becomes, the vitality of *quality* will elude it. However complex the binary world of 'either-*or*' becomes, our human ability to grasp a paradox, an 'either-*and*', will elude it. We are human when we embrace the *messiness* of life and its infinite gradations. We can take our human messy *quality* into a realm built of numbers and try to hold our own. This book is about the challenges in doing so, and some of the problems that arise when we fail to hold our own. Upsets and new social norms have always accompanied new technologies. We all join together in determining what form these will take through how we think about and respond to them. One quality to which quantity is utterly irrelevant is *the quality of you*, which you determine when you act with conscious freedom amidst the bewildering new possibilities of technological change.

I wish to offer some advice, which has been gathered from others and developed through my own reflections, on how to go safely with freedom in the digital realm. If this realm proves to be a truly great gift to humanity, then here are skills which you may still need in order to remain awake and aware in it. If it turns out to be a hell, here's some practical advice on how to prevent getting too burned. This book is about holding your own in the digital realm while its changes swirl around you. Some say it is a losing battle. That is not helpful. Surely, we are here to meet whatever comes towards us with all the consciousness we can muster.

As you can see, this book celebrates what it criticizes. Inside it you'll find exercises to help you use digital means for *your* ends, to overcome the tiredness and fly above the digital sea like an eagle when you choose to, or dive into it with mastery like a dolphin. The exercises begin with '**Try this**'. You can just read those exercises. There are many points of entry and exit. Read it from cover to cover, surf it, use bits of it, re-order it. Use what works for you.

An invitation to hurl this book away

If you have no problem with the effects of digital technologies and social media platforms, if you do not feel the negative 'drag' and have no fears of losing a part of yourself in them, then read no further. Put the book down, give it away or recycle it somehow. If you happen to be a champion of total surrender to the miracle of digital technology, then this book will irritate you and make no apology for having done so. This isn't a book to convert you.

If you can't *not* answer the phone when it rings and you spend 40 hours a week on social media and you read your texts instead of kissing your partner goodnight and you don't give your kids real attention because you just *have to* prioritize new responses to your tweet, then you are in the first level of hell, the place of Wretched Contentment. If you want to regain something which you feel you've lost to the digital realm, then this book is for you. It deliberately repeats itself from different points of view. It is in two parts. Part One is an overview of the digital realm's territory and of some of its challenges. Part Two develops themes set out in Part One and dives in more deeply.

PART ONE

1

The Problem and the Challenge

The digital realm has existed since human beings began to use numbers for understanding and representing real things, such as natural objects and the processes between them. Since its advent in the form of electronic media it has transformed the world in the blink of an eye.

The pioneers of digital computing, working in research establishments and laboratories, wanted to connect and share their knowledge in ways that didn't need physical journeys and face-to-face meetings. They also wanted to avoid the inefficiencies of paper-based information. The first version of the internet was conceived, as far back as the 1940s and 1950s, as a medium through which academics and scientists could collaborate. That technical capability exploded all over a post-war world fairly itching for newness and choice when Sir Tim Berners-Lee, a computer scientist and professor at MIT, had the notion of bringing it to the rest of us, in the form of the World Wide Web.

Before the web made connectivity between widely separated computers possible, some of us were zapping aliens on the first personal computers. As a 15-year-old, I spent hours on my Acorn Electron computer, playing adventure games and tenpin bowling with red square dots. Many of the popular early computer games soon offered more – alternative worlds in which aliens were real and where we could govern our own country. I remember being addicted to a game called *1984* in which I was the prime minister.

The first computer game is often credited as being *Spacewar*, from Steve Russell at MIT. We were offered simple shoot-'em-ups and text-based adventures: 'You make your third wish and take off, gliding into the sky.' They offered interactive stories in which we were the hero, able to choose actions and to experience the outcomes which were programmed into the game. When we had done something right, the feedback gave us a high. 'You put the gold in your knapsack and gain 10 points.' Years before the emergence of the internet and social media, these were the first 'likes'. We played in order to progress. We had the thrill of a little victory via a quicker and easier route than becoming proficient at a real sport or meeting some fascinating person at a real party.

Text games soon became two-dimensional, graphics-based, and then went into three dimensions. A few years later our game character was rendered in cartoon-like or lifelike graphics. A couple of decades after that we began to inhabit a virtual reality (a kind of reality in effect, but not in fact). We could create simulated models of all kinds of things, such as flying a jet plane or running the government. A dual experience of physical and virtual worlds was emerging. Objects, landscapes and rules in the virtual world were versions of physical reality – an interesting mix of both the fantastic and mundane. Some years later, virtual worlds such as *Second Life* and *Minecraft* led to literally millions of children and adults 'zoning out' of physical life for hours each day. Many children cut their teeth on digital worlds such as *The Sims*.

Chips constantly became smaller and processing faster and cheaper. Newer gadgets offered ever more colourful, flexible and exciting versions of mundane reality. This realm was not constrained by the limitations of scale of the real world. We could not only create a new world but there were no limits to how fast we could travel in it, how big it could get and how the laws of nature applied. We could transform ourselves into a fox. We may not fly like an eagle in our physical bodies but in a virtual realm we would soon be able to fly as freely as we wished. People flocked to the new worlds. When *Second Life* was first developed, it had so many users and financial activity (buying and selling land, products and services, real as well as digital) that Reuters sent in a full-time reporter to report news of it back to the real world and vice versa. His name was Adam Reuters.

These visions of the future fuelled the flames of the digital inferno. Behind all of that was a technology which used an artificial language for writing programs; these represent sequences of minute electrical switches set in silicon. The programs were brought to electronic life for us through interfaces and screens of all kinds. Each tiny switch is, like any switch, either on or off, and the great challenge was to create for the end-user an experience of infinite and flowing possibilities from sequences of current changes from on to off and from off to on. It has obviously been a runaway technological success.

For some, the next plan is to realize something which science fiction imagined a century ago – to *port* our consciousness into a virtual and better world and truly 'fly'. In this scenario, technology solves the problem of human frailty by enhancing it or even by rendering our physical form superfluous by a transfer of human consciousness into immortal digital reality. Perhaps feeding that dream is another one, of solving our material problems by creating a virtual reality with unlimited resources – we have only to find a way to minimize our bodily function and transpose ourselves into another realm of computer-realized imagination.

Many programmers found an artificial world into which they could escape, and many of us followed them. We indulged ourselves in the realms of fantasy and first-person role play games. The image of the computer genius behind these games, as captured in popular films such as *War Games* and *Independence Day*, was that of an introvert seeking escape from an unfriendly world into an anonymous virtual world. The lone geek lacks the hero's looks and emotional literacy, probably due to a lack of time spent in real social interaction, but he gets to play the greatest game of all, that of saving the world. Sure, not all programmers fulfilled *that* stereotype but many were deeply attracted to a virtual world and the possibility of leaving the rest behind. Not surprisingly, many 'techies' with a profound wish to escape were drawn to science fantasy. The fantasy virtual worlds of Larry Niven, Isaac Asimov, Tolkien and Robert Heinlein already offered magical or technological utopias and dystopias. The 'holodeck', the lived dream world and other parallel universes were going to take us to places that were richer in colour and broader in possibility. Losing oneself in these worlds was soon a widespread pursuit, and it still is for vast numbers of us.

The roots of the digital realm which we experience are within the minds of the original programmers and designers. Many of them were loners who found a home in the world of computing and in working environments that were one-on-one with a computer – informal, with no need for office uniform and supplied with unlimited sweets and cola. Departments of information technology and computer engineering became the ivory towers of social avoidance. I've met many examples of this type over the years. I have, of course, met computer engineers who are socially literate and emotionally warm but there is a real core of avoiders who have shaped the digital realm for the purpose of doing without the complication of actually meeting. Almost the whole of the digital realm is still based on that foundation: when we are *virtual* we no longer need to meet face to face.

Email was a virtual version of the physical memo, fax and letter. People often printed out all of their emails at work, just in case. That still goes on but, for the rest of us, keeping all of our letters in a place that doesn't require bulky physical storage is a dream come true. Email was a perfect way to communicate, without eye contact and the other hazards of physical presence. It was only one step from linear emailing – from one computer to certain other ones – to chat rooms in which we could converse with many other people without needing to be physically present. We added video and then *avatars*, or digital version of ourselves. This presented the possibility of renaming ourselves and becoming another version of ourselves. We could not merely escape from others; we could escape from ourselves as well. The online self could experiment with being more confident and socially extroverted. When online, shy quiet Kevin would become his avatar, bold *Thor352*, a roaring warrior with powerful fists.

We were offered another mode of existence, a virtual life rooted in fantasies. For those seeking escape from the pressure and the immediacy of staring eyes the digital realm was too good to resist. It offered simplicity. We could get the treasure without any physical risk at all. We could get new lives in which to replay our failures with different outcomes. We could explore new behaviours without the complications. We could flirt and threaten without consequence. We could 'have' other lives in which we could stretch the boundaries of behaviour. We could kill people and be rewarded with 50 bonus points.

But did this online role-play lead to more confident behaviours in real life? In some cases, perhaps it did. In many cases, it led to people being split between virtual-confident and real-shy and even to keeping online behaviour secret from real friends.

As computers came to be all about 'going online' a new frontier society emerged which was like the Wild West, lawless and exciting, and many staked a claim in it. The rest of us, the 'masses', tended to follow along, bemused. We were invited to join in, get online, take part and make this miracle grow. We 'entered' the digital realm and withdrew from the more subtle and far less predictable physical world.

We might do well to note that the need for social adjustment must have accompanied the development of earlier technologies, such as writing, painting and printing. With printing, information became available which had previously been hidden away; and entering into books or paintings meant immersion in something that was very different to whatever it was in reality they represented. Since we do not spread our attention when we are focused, being 'in there' really means not being out here. However, it is really hard to separate the positive potential of a new technology that overcomes the need to travel, that quickens the flow of information and helps to get things done from its potential to get so many of us to spend so much time channelling some abstract part of ourselves through a digital interface. Reality changes at that interface, or perhaps it is better to say that it is lost – the sharp intake of breath, another person's vital reaction and the challenges of being exposed are all filtered out. Life is no longer *live*. Our text conversations become like drama scripts, and the *smileys* are ready-made simplistic stage directions for a script that is rarely played out in physical reality.

We now inhabit game worlds that are so badly imagined and realized that we have to accept something pretty mediocre in order to gain value from them. Due to its fixed, artificial bounds, the computer game is deeply repetitive by its very nature. The most elaborate virtual world role play game is still only a face-painted version of the old computer tennis game *Pong*. The clever graphics and animations still require profound suspension of disbelief. (I know this because I have played them all.) This has often been secretly confessed to me by digital players; openly, we have to play along with it and defend the blandness. If we complain we are seen as betrayers of the cause. Almost every online game is still binary, as was *Pong*, requiring us to kill or be killed, pretend to be somewhere, left, right, forward, backwards, because the universe of possibilities in a virtual reality is a closed one. Action games have, however, developed in many ways. Nowadays many of them present an astonishing variety of intriguing moving images which cannot be seen in ordinary reality. If you utterly surrender to them, and become as immersed as your taste for fantasy will let you, then the highs and lows can be powerful enough to rival an evening out with your friends. And thus we re-calibrate experience – our digital 'wow' moments feel more valuable only because we have forgotten what the utter beauty and mystery of nuanced humanity can offer us. We compare the garish of the latest version to the grey of the old version instead of to the subtle glory of the evening sky.

The best games can now replicate those shades – the birdsong, the swish of the wind and their mysterious effect on our moods and our dreams — at least well enough for those willing to be seduced by a digital counterfeit. Many games are full of wit, music and sound effects that are of top quality and display an artistry that is often beautiful. But, as technology currently stands, as we step into its digital world we are only *sitting down* to a so-called quest as limited as a 'choose your own adventure' book. What becomes of the quests and surprises of the real world, and its real rent to be paid and its real children to be lovingly put to bed? In moments of honesty, committed game players have revealed to me what the gaming experience has brought them. Some have pointed to significant highs and moments of celebration but the vast majority, over the long run, express disappointment that the games have mostly been a distraction which took up months of their time. These games are built on repetition and are finally disappointing when the simulation reaches its boundary and cracks at the 'edges'. One player said to me: 'I've realized, it's all so much dope.' Another said: 'You have to really immerse yourself for long periods to get the benefit.' And another: 'It gets a bit samey after a time; it's mostly better graphics.' Finally: 'At one point I only went out to get more food and beer. I didn't shave and the only people I interacted with were online and I killed a few of those.' I've also spoken to a huge number of people who describe some of their digital experience as being real. When I spent time looking at *Second Life* I encountered people who were 'there' for many hours a day because 'there' was better than 'here'. I met people who felt empowered by it and who felt they had found friends they had been seeking all their lives. Many had reinvented themselves. Their 'avatar' in *Second Life* was better looking, younger and more socially outgoing. Here in Brighton, UK, I know many of my 'friends' on *Facebook* personally. A great number of them appear, in their digital guises, to be more relaxed, confident versions of their originals. Unfortunately, the originals, after their virtual reinvention, seem no more confident in a real room with real people. Sometimes their self-possession seems undermined by involuntary mannerisms — a frequent use of a thumbs-up accompanied by 'kewl'. Back in reality the fall seems profound, because *Facebook* is not getting them work in acting or finding them that elusive agent, and because tweeting is rarely selling tickets for their shows.

If the benefit sought is escape, then the digital realm may well be beneficial, just as long as you are in it. It was fashioned for this purpose far more than as a means of enhancing the real social condition. There must be exceptions to this. Children might be more confident as a result of social networking. They *might* learn to be more collaborative as a result of using collaborative software in their learning at school, but digital social time largely delivers benefits only when we are engaged in digital activity. Shy people, I would suggest, become no less shy in the real world after engaging in extrovert behaviour online. The shyness can be even more pro-found when they are back in a real room with real eyes looking at them.

This, of course, could all be changed. We could imagine the digital realm in terms of smart and conscious enhancements to the steps we take in the real world. At present it is a huge market of time-using escapism. Artificial virtual worlds are offered up to us on a plate and they lock too many of us into repetitive and mediocre experiences. We can have, it seems, more friends than ever, as long as we don't meet them in the real world (at least not very often). We can like them, hug them, send them birthday cards (and we don't even need to attend their party and bring a real present). But most of our friends on *Facebook* are not friends at all, as many have discovered when *Facebook* friends don't show up to their real world events or respond to requests for tangible help.

At the core of it all is a failure of imagination so tragic that we can't bear to see it, let alone name it for what it is. Our phones are poor tools when used as cameras but we view so much of our experience – the people we share our best times with, our encounters with animals and breathtaking countryside – by peer-ing at them on our phone camera viewfinders. They produce, with little skilled input from us, either accidental masterpieces or another blurred cat. (Many of us have spent thousands of pounds on phones with cameras that still can't take a decent photo indoors in low light.) Then, in the aftermath of a sacred physical moment, we are 'posting' our images online and checking in to see who 'liked' it. We go online every few minutes because we don't want to 'miss out', and we miss the rare breathtaking moment unfolding in front of us. Sure, immediate connection and feedback are gratifying in their way. But what do we lose? We visit a waterfall and hardly see it. What we see when we are looking at the pictures of it in a digital album is a very different thing.

What does all this virtual bashing lead to? To this: I never can 'go online', at least, not as a whole person. There is no 'cloud', and our second lives are a poor rendering of our first lives. When I sit before a computer, I sit before another kind of phenomenon. I can activate aspects of its potential and allow things to emerge from it but there is no magical door for me to walk through and no possibility of escape into it. But then, digital life doesn't need to be about mindless liking and escape. It doesn't have to be a derivative rendition of sci-fi fantasy worlds. We can meet it as simply an artificial medium galvanized by electricity. It will continue to be an increasingly complex imagined virtual reality, yet it will continue to be virtual. When we drive the virtual car, the car isn't moving anywhere, and nor are we. It sits square in the middle of the screen as images of the landscape moving past us mimic sense perceptions which our real bodies must have learned through experiencing real movement. It all happens in a fashion which, because we do not understand its inner structure, is seemingly miraculous. To know it as a rendering of living reality and as an imagination in code is not at all to condemn it, only to put it in perspective. To know it consciously in this way breaks the spell and helps us become more awake to it. The digital realm is a copy which can trick us. When we surrender to that trick, we can gain highs of different kinds, but we can also surrender to a tragic over-simplicity. After a while our surrender can become habitual. Our expectations are lowered and important parts of reality seem too difficult. We lose the healthy taste for it. Why meet when you can call? Why call when you can text? Why eat out when you can order online with free delivery? Why go there when you can watch it in 3D? Why work on that friendship when you can get a hundred 'likes' in five minutes on *Facebook*?

We might come to suspect all those images which are so insistently served up for our consumption. We might remind ourselves just how limited the digital realm is; we can still play in there, but when we are wide awake. I promise you, that is going to be far better than sleepy surrender to it.

We haven't even sketched out all the adjustments we need to make. And it is time we did or we'll soon find the virtual world is making us ill. We will need to make even greater adjustments as newer technologies descend upon us or we'll be encased in technology. We already speak of computer *memory* and personify the machine whenever we say that *it thinks*. So how do we now imagine computer 'intelligence'? Different answers to that huge little question are part of a struggle for our image of what a human being actually is – an input-output system with a processing unit and a display, or something entirely different in kind and operating within different forces? We largely imagine it in the form of a cyborg rather than in the form of a pure machine – that is, as computerized attachments to a living being, the one thing which actually has consciousness. We may well plug in more and more, and link our nerve endings to processors and sensors and gradually turn into the Tin Man in *The Wizard of Oz*, yearning for a heart. Attempts to create digital versions of human existence will seriously hold us back.

The future

A newer generation of programmers and designers sees things differently. It has a love for real life and sees computing as a servant of mankind. This emerging generation of *digerati* is mindful and not escapist by nature. They don't want us always 'in there', always on, unless it is with a sense of willed purpose. These folk, who have grown up in the digital age, are not the technical, cold caricatures of Generation Y. They reject the old metaphors, which see the computer as an extension of office paraphernalia with its desktop and inboxes every bit as cluttered as the real desk. They want to reshape it. Many to whom I have spoken view human freedom and the evolution of culture as key elements within a new relation to the digital realm. To enter 'The Matrix' isn't their goal. The digital playground, for them, isn't so much a place *in which* we play but a place we play *out of.*

Some people I've met say it isn't possible to remain free in the digital inferno and that ultimately we will be swallowed up by it. Possibly. It is easy to see the danger creeping in when one's hand is drawn slavishly to an incoming call, as if welcoming the interruption. Whatever metaphors underpin the digital realm – from desktop to cloud – real life is only in the real world. Some of us will die young and others not till they are old. Others are alone, while others are in the midst of warm friends and family. We sit on trains, lie on sofas, breathe and frown. We laugh and we fear. Our real world is not a metaphor, as real joy and pain confirm. We are in that world and digital interaction can both help and harm us.

The situation requires humans who know themselves to be the agents, feeding in something that eludes the machine – the power of human imagination. Our imagination produces what and who we will be. It is a product of our growth, our chaos and our fear, our subtlety and nuance, of the alchemy of mortal flesh and transcendent dreaming. And we are set apart from the computer's mimicry of intelligence by one thing – our clumsiness. Our ideas may be clumsy and not as perfectly structured as a program might be but, unlike the program, they are not confined within explicit parameters. Moreover, only humans have ideas. Within our clumsiness is our ability to learn by finding relations between ideas without needing, as a computer does, totally exhaustive criteria for doing so. We do not learn as well when we say 'it is either this or that', as if seeing the significance of something were merely sorting through the mutually exclusive possibilities. We learn more effectively when we look for the grey areas, the ambiguities and new relations between things, as we do when we understand humour and meta-phor – as a child can do easily and well before it uses the simplest bit of explicit reasoning. Anyway, life isn't two valued: either/or, on/off, true/false. Such a formal limitation can help in basic mathematics and building sequences of switches, but it is just the beginning when it comes to cooking, exploring, painting and play. We find relations not only between existing ideas but through play we create new ideas with new relations between them. A computer never had an idea. Neither can it say 'I' to itself with the wordless will which is our true individuality. We will retain our self-aware-ness in the digital world only if we distinguish our inner will from a lifeless machine and act accordingly. Even though the machine can far outstrip us in speed and the range of data it can be programmed to correlate, it is human ideas and human will which are causally upstream of any action performed by a machine. So, we rightly laugh at clumsy clowns because they reveal the thing of value which is essential in all of us.

The technical geniuses will make progress in getting machines to copy this fuzzier part of human consciousness. Algorithms that are closer to the more inductive and clumsier learning of humans will no doubt be announced as breakthroughs in artificial intelligence but most likely they will use generalizations based on analysis of enormous samples of patterns of human behaviour gathered from our online activity and input.

Our clumsiness and creative imagination are our priceless value. When it comes to developments in processing, we get in the way. Computers are faster at calculating and cross-referring than us but they lack the miraculous clumsiness which we have for getting brand new ideas. Mere processing doesn't need human clumsiness trying to micro-manage it, or to be 'in' it. Human intervention will actually retard some of the new programs which are self-correcting and can interact with other programs. Our place is on the outside, with the mental vision and the physical hands for taking the results to physical realization.

In future this will be even more the case. Once many machines and the separate platforms are mutually compatible (through a universal digital language) they will be able to join up and correlate their vast stores of data. This will be the *semantic web*, the web in dialogue with itself. A kind of universal internal conversation will take place between sections within the web itself. Humans can slow processing down in a way which misses out on some of its potential. For example, *Twitter* can take a snapshot of what a whole community is thinking at a point in time. This emerges from millions of tweets which are analysed to show real-time trends of thought and opinion across millions of independent minds. No human being, even a team of human beings, could read and correlate so many single tweets to show us, as it is happening, what the computer search program can.

There will be a vast realm of content. It goes in raw but when it links with other content a kind of semantic dance can begin. One sentence links to another, images merge to give new images, a database links to symptoms, a diagnostic analysis results in thera-peutic suggestion. It's all happening 'underneath the bonnet' with vast databases cross-referring at great speed.

We'll do the input and reap the output. Experts will swoop in and out but the sheer complexity of the exchange between databases and machines will be beyond a single person. We might imagine a digital realm guided by the one thing it lacks: consciousness which is alive, as no computer is. Then we'll leave the computers to get on with it, setting safety limits to protect ourselves. The internet will dialogue internally, in a realm where people, aeroplanes, hotel bookings, codes and scripts will all intermingle as digital words and phrases. And the emerging meanings (according to the inventors) of the semantic web will open up a new world for us.

Something new may be beginning here … the digital realm becoming a place where our imagination is the guiding force. We will be connected but not lost in it. The internet will become a tool of consciousness rather than a space for passively being in. Just imagine that for a moment, just as a possibility, and test it against your instincts and intuition. We aren't really supposed to be spending hours staring at screens pursuing digital versions of what we could be doing together, face to face. We probably should not be 'in there' much, if at all. The internet is there to help us cure cancer and research sustainable ways of making things. It is there to help us store things. It's there to challenge us with new data and new answers to the questions we put to it. Are we really supposed to be lumbering around in it, poking at each other and sharing photos of places we hardly saw with our own physical eyes?

So where does this imagination lead? I think it leads to an as yet unimagined digital realm, one foreshadowed by the notion of the semantic web. I think it leads to possible new directions for computing that are more based on verb and process than noun and place.

It won't be about desktops, but about helping content to dance, first with our help, and then in and with itself.

It will be about gaining insight from the dance of content.

It will be about leaving binary inevitability behind – to *like* or not to *like* without nuance – and working again with the painful challenge of a real range of responses.

As in physical reality, we'll seek for the quality of quality, not only its quantity. It will be about engagement and disengagement in different ways. It will be about finding the gestures in the movement and interaction of content.

We can – probably will – create avatars to operate according to more sophisticated behavioural models, a kind of digital puppetry.

But computing will not attempt to render consciousness nor be a virtual haven for social avoiders. It will be a tool that enhances this world. We will return to ourselves, the alive and creative clumsy imaginers. It is just beginning.

Now, I know how weird that all sounds. I don't understand it all myself. I gave myself permission to imagine a digital realm that didn't try to ape human behaviour in its limited digital way. I took away our clumsiness and imagined a digital world that could be programmed to develop itself out of itself. As the digital realm is developing it is starting to upgrade itself without human intervention. We input the design for something and it prints in three dimensions, adjusting, refining and even arriving at new variations. Some of our biggest challenges – climate, disease – will find solutions through programs that go well beyond the small causal chains and the few factors which human minds can contain. It is the program that writes a new program that writes a new program that might yield vital data for our real world. It will be programmed to question and challenge us, change program settings benevolently and automatically, and even use scripts we don't fully understand. As things are, the monster on the slab isn't quite behaving as planned. When content is programmed to interact with other content, then what emerges might terrify us, and it might delight us.

The sheep and the goats

Above all, a new realm may emerge inspired by human creativity and imagination, though it could of course go several ways. The signs, for a split into several groups of people on quite different evolutionary roads, are already there. On one road will be those who dream of *porting* their consciousness into digital immortality. But, in essence, we never are our avatars. It is not that one day we could be, but that we shouldn't even try to be. On another road might be those who retreat into a holier-than-thou rejection of everything digital. Then there will be the new *technosophists*, or wise technologists, who stand free and use technology creatively to benefit the one world which counts.

We don't have to merely react. We can direct our experience of it.

Learning the spider dance

A few years ago I wrote a short play called *Text*. It was a series of scenes between a man and a woman. They had been in a relationship for several years and a decline had set in. As physical intimacy lessened they attempted to compensate by texting more and more. The text kisses were now exceeding the number of physical kisses. The play attempted to show the importance of the physical connection between us and explores disasters that occur when we assume things about people with whom we have mostly digital relationships. It didn't end happily. Understandably, the play was definitely biased in favour of physical kisses. In most scenes the *X*s and the texts are substitutions for their physical relationship. In one scene each one types an *X* to the other – that and nothing more. He is on a train, she is at home. They are both affected and they both smile. The technology symbolizes an act that requires physical presence and therefore has to be imagined. The *X* is a token of the person imagining the act of kissing. They each feel the lack of the other but, inside, they can consciously will their imagining out across physical space. The device delivers the *X*, but the bit which matters – the will force of each person – isn't in or on the screen but willed and sent as a gesture across space. The kiss is meant and is an authentic gesture. It's the only scene that shows how technology can serve us, but it does so only if we maintain and affirm our relations within physical space. The technology then serves the gesture. When the gesture is received it can be trusted, and turned back into what the sender meant, which was a real imagining of a kiss – all of this tends to happen more when it is done slowly, with conscious will and intentions which express the feelings we have for the other person.

How does that scenario compare to most texting, typed lightning fast and phrased in the language of 'awesome' and 'Kewl!'? Now there's nothing absolutely wrong about lightning fast chat. Indeed, the technologies of instant messaging are available for playful interaction 24/7. What I beg you to consider here is that our sacred moments just don't render well into set-piece phrases and smileys.

At an instinctive level we know this and compensate with extra payments at the virtual exchange rate where a real kiss is converted to ten virtual kisses and 'good', said face to face, becomes 'awesome' by text. But the gestures we send across space can be sacred and vital to us and these need our own inner activity to maintain their worth and integrity. The digital device is a ready means for sending our words and images but for our experience of it to be authentic and not feel devalued we have to summon up the inner gesture and send it with warmth of purpose to the other person. We can do this. We do not have to go into automatic behaviour mode with a little device which we love using for its own sake. It might feel like a trivial distinction. I think it counts for everything. And when the other person knows and trusts we are doing this, the smiles and inner feelings are real and heartfelt.

But *Text* was not a negative judgement on digital interaction. In one short scene, a simple message of 'I miss you' drew 'I miss you' in response, and it was a moment of tenderness. The missing was deeply felt, not concocted for the sake of having something to say. 'I miss you' is empty without the inner invisible gesture being felt and trusted on both sides. In *Text* the technology became a medium of *conscious* communication. The scene showed that when we know what motives live in us, and we choose motives which are ours, then we have a chance of making technology serve us. The gadget should be the thing which we use rather than, as Jaron Lanier warns us, the thing we are becoming. For us to merge with our gadgets is, I believe, the intention of the corporations behind the technology. The images so nicely pictured in their advertising act as our motives for being *always-on* and pressing send, send, send.

Text also examined what I call 'fingertip connection'. As part of the research for the play, we came across some film of an African jumping spider. As it moves, its front legs move in a way which looks uncannily like thumb texting – fast, furious but very controlled and functional. Spiders move a bit like our hands move across a keyboard or a screen keypad. The image said something useful, I thought, and we incorporated some of that film into the theatre performance, overlaying the spider onto the texting thumbs of one of the actors. It was an almost perfect match!

When I was a child my mother taught secretarial skills at a local school. I remember, while watching my mother's lightning fast fingertips, being amazed and a bit scared of whatever aspect of my gentle mother it was that sent letters flying across a page that quickly. Typing at 60 words per minute and taking shorthand at 120 words per minute looked remarkably like the moving legs and pincers of a spider. In the science fiction magazines I read as a child (I collected some dating from as far back as the 1930s and even made my own versions of them), many of the aliens were portrayed as spider-like beings and all of them were remarkably clever. They had huge heads and pincers like surgical instruments. So often, in the magazines, these beings had a cold intellect and a deadness of heart which, I now realize, was meant to be impressive in some way. Spiders weave webs to ensnare other creatures in order to eat them. How smoothly it spins and how efficiently the web pattern emerges! If we personify this genius for pure pattern we arrive at a being which is a cold and purely calculating intellect. This is an image of power. The prey is weaker and so is caught in the web and its efforts to disentangle itself result in becoming more tied up than before, until it finally 'submits'.

The primary metaphor that characterizes online digital interaction is the web. Social networking is about making connections, signing up, inviting and joining. The network is a complex set of interlinking strands, woven by us within the underlying network and databases. Are we the spiders? Are we its strands, along which moves the consciousness of other beings? Are we the prey? In Mark Slouka's *The Assault on Reality*, it is we who are caught in the web.

The creator, or the spider, is the corporation. In this image for the web, users are mostly passive and their actions limited to responding to prompts.

In Jaron Lanier's book *You Are Not a Gadget*, one can see the sense in which we are the gadgets and the corporation is the user of gadgets. We text because the corporation uses us to text. We think we are acting, but usually we are reacting. The corporation needs us to be 'always on'. It has given us a way to talk as quickly as a spider can walk, and to send messages as fast as a spider can spin a thread. We are offered a way to do it with superfast thinking via lightning-quick thumb and fingertips. (Some children can thumb text without even taking their phones out of their pockets.) But it is alarming that there's no time for us to feel what we mean to say. Feeling in the human heart prompts some reflective pause to take the measure of something we value, but any pause in superfast thinking feels like sluggishness. It isn't, as we will get to later, but it feels like it. Superfast tap-tap-tap goes with cold calculation, shorthand and minimal touch. No time to consider or empathize. Type fast. Think with the speed of a reflex. Be like a scuttling spider. We can tap glass with the ends of fingertips and write a sentence in seconds. Speed creates efficiency and a digital version of speed-of-sound physical running. Our words reach the other in a second, faster than we can speak the words. No larynx is needed, no tongue, no lips. Those soft organs mysteriously create physical sounds which carry as much feeling as thought. It used to be our main medium. Now we prefer to be like something with a large head and little arms and legs coming directly out of it which taper into long fingertips that can tap screens and point like a clever spider. From a distance it looks like a dance. In *Text*, we used pizzicato violin music behind the tap-tap-tapping of the jumping spider and its effect was comic and grotesque.

Responding with feeling involves a pause and drawing up something from within, as if we were trying to see with our heart. Our response is not merely a development of the linear logic of the conversation. We allow the effect of the words to work on us and we respond out of that feeling. Try it. It is harder to feel like that if you are staring at the screen with your fingers poised to strike. Look away. The pensive look away, of someone drawing some feeling towards herself, is often captured in old paintings. The pause in the drama allows things to sink in; the silence between the notes gives music its meaning. And, often, a response born of feeling is different to one born of thinking only. Perhaps we fear those responses. Is it easier just to use our heads?

In the many workshops I have facilitated over the years all over the world (especially in working environments) it was accepted that the predominance of the intellect over feeling existed in the workplace before computers came along. Feeling at work was unpredictable, slow and unprofessional. Whenever I asked people how they felt about an issue or question, they would invariably begin the reply with, 'I think'. And, 'I think I feel' is not the same as 'I feel'. I believe that we limit our range of responses because we have technologized the way we consider things; fast equals clever, but it also equals one-dimensional and, in that case, maybe not so clever.

We've made it easier to bypass feeling by creating fingertip communication. Smartphones these days have applications for going straight from speech to text. It isn't hugely reliable but it makes for a very different kind of digital experience.

Try this: reacting from the heart

When you next receive a text that prompts some emotional reaction in you, read it carefully and then listen for what your heart is saying. Search within for how you feel about the content of that text. *Hold the other person in mind* and reach out for what you believe is in his or her heart. Then form a reply. You can then dictate it into the phone (if you have the right application), say it aloud or voice it in your head before you type and send. You might find that the slower response is less cold, more eloquent and more 'you'.

Fingertip connection. Is it really any different from speaking with our own lips and drawing upon the rhythm of breath? At one level, of course it is different. It is physically different. But is anything really lost, and is anything new gained when we connect digitally?

Over the last ten years I have examined my own texts and the texts sent by others, from friends, family, colleagues. I've also asked a huge number of people from different age groups, backgrounds and walks of life how they experience texting. Without a doubt, they say, there's the benefit of immediacy. Conversations can take place across vast distances at little or no cost. We can share thoughts and feelings via words, emotional icons, images and, more recently, decent quality video (with holograms soon to come). Many people have told me that a more confident self is released in them when they send a text or message via social media. It is a new art form that we have only begun to explore. Some texters, status updaters, tweeters and micro-bloggers rival Oscar Wilde with their wit. Well, surprise, surprise, there's a dark side to that. The heavy breathing anonymous phone caller also gets a kind of confidence from hiding behind non-physical presence. We fire off texts more readily because they bypass the complicated thoughts and feelings which show on our faces. A smiley can be a simple way of communicating, but it can also be a mask. Hiding behind masks can be delightful at a masquerade, but it makes for a very different day-to-day world.

We can sometimes experience friends as positive or confident online only to find that they can't deliver on the online persona when face to face. This creates a double standard, of incongruence and even two-facedness. Some would suggest that this is something new and valuable, not something to be concerned about. Digital interaction releases the caged bird in us. It helps the shy to be more confident by allowing them to experiment with a more confident version of themselves while online. Yet that could also prevent them from developing that quality over time. Each one of us is our life-time's work. The problem with putting an elevator on a children's climbing frame is that it removes the opportunity to develop climbing skills. From this point of view, our weaknesses, or at least some of them, really are our development opportunities. Does digital short-cutting steal from us our chance to become stronger and more skilled in the real world? And does doing what we find easier in the short term stunt important lifetime growth?

Evolution has a way of making what we don't use, or no longer need, shrivel and die in the long run. We evolve in the direction of need and usefulness. Will we lose our vocal cords, grow longer fingers with hardened skin on their tips? Of course, technology may soon render fingertip communication obsolete with the result that other parts of us fall into disuse. So, much depends on what direction technology takes. It may not be long before fingertips on gorilla glass are outmoded. Yet, in all possible scenarios, if someone said you'll become cleverer but colder like a spider, would you choose that road? For your children, for your grandchildren?

When we get a smiley, do we feel authentically smiled at?

XXXXXXXXX at the end of a text is a kind of desperate way to compensate for the coldness of the medium. When we get a hug in brackets, or as a smiley, we don't feel hugged. We rarely feel an impulse of warmth from the sender. We imagine it if we deeply need it and we can talk our heart into believing the digital hug is real. But wishful thinking and self-delusion are not ideal ways to manage our mental and emotional lives. Now, before you accuse me of missing the point I have a confession to make: I am deliberately missing the point. Of course, all that is too negative – what that view shows is the importance of follow-through with warmth and authenticity. Of course a smiley isn't a real smile. It's something different and new. To compare it to a real smile is silly and unfair. Of course an *X* isn't usually a real kiss. It's a digital form of positivity – again, something new. It coincides with its physical counterparts and is not meant to replace them. The overlap is simply one of designed familiarity. Am I a dinosaur, an old fuddy-duddy who hasn't understood the new world of the playful avatar with its creative opportunities of projecting strong social gestures into a virtual social space that makes them playful, lighter, ironic and less intense?

Now we can kiss without the complication of physicality. And plenty of people are kissing and hugging in the digital world who are not doing that in the real world. Yes, we gain something new; indeed, what we gain can feel refreshing, uplifting and enlivening and we can want more and more of it. We get uncomplicated impact, simple effectiveness, instant 'touch'; we get easy reach, and bare minimum, often upbeat response. We can get to a wow moment by simply posting a picture and, within minutes or even seconds, 50 people in our *Facebook* world have given us a 'like'. (Note: on *Facebook* there are no dislike buttons; maybe their research taught them we are more likely to keep coming back if it makes us feel good.) I have posted, as an experiment, nonsense phrases, terrible photos and the most awful poem I could write. I almost instantly received 'likes' from people, at least some of whom I know are never so generous when face to face.

But will a dose of healthy criticism spoil the digital party? In the digital world, where we publish our thoughts, photos and diary entries for online friends, it seems to be fairly unacceptable to criticize. (There is, of course, all the savage criticism on the anonymous sites, which I suppose must be a sign of letting a different kind of human weakness off the leash.) There is almost blanket praise for whatever we share. This is not because the content itself is so praiseworthy — indeed it often truly isn't — but because affirmation is almost more important than intelligent engagement. It's a thumbs-up for investing another minute of life online. Proof of this can be found in announcing events on social media. I've seen theatre productions financially ruined because they naively believed that the 200 people who said they were coming to the show would actually do so. This is because the commitment isn't to the physical world, but to the digital action which has been shared. 'I'm attending' means 'I'm attending your digital event – I'm showing up to your announcement.' It is a commitment to the positive intention, not the action. What we get in the digital realm is a lot of digital affirmation and avatar approval. What we lose is the connection with real world commitment to action. In the digital realm, intention and aspiration are virtual acts. Digital interaction is about actions that are hoped for. Often our actions are played out metaphors. Shy people play-act at being extrovert, with smileys and capitals in bold and they attend digital events with thumbs-up affirmation, with comments on threads, tagging, regular nudging and adding to this and that. Activity appears on a published time-line to remind us of our productivity in the digital realm. Everything we do, just about every click, is big news, enough for a public announcement. We default to getting email reminders of each action unless we know how to switch notifications off. I've met a lot of people who have inboxes stuffed with notifications from some-where or other and have given up trying to find out where the settings are to switch them off. You are automatically included whether you want it or not, and then it's up to you to exit. Your exit prompts an 'Are you sure?' email followed by a 'We're sorry to see you go' email to tire us out a bit more and make us feel like party poopers. Inclusion is affirmation. Voluntary exclusion is digital party-pooping.

Here the skill is simply to step through, with a will towards something else, leaving the digital events behind. We are back to intuition again, or at least that part of it which lives deep inside, in our will. How much time are you wasting on digital partying? How much of it adds to your development and personality, or to your sense of self-realization and purpose? And how much of it is so much gap-filling because you've lost connection to the things which require getting off the sofa and out of the house? Has a walk by the sea become a chore? Are lunch breaks too tiring because they might leave you alone with your thoughts, or alone with your colleagues?

We can slide easily into the digital inferno and have a warm (often lukewarm) digital bathe whenever we choose. With the advent of mobile devices we don't even need to power up a computer. It is there instantly. Soon, with developments in wearable digital technology, it will all appear unbidden, overlaying the experience of our physical senses. And when distraction becomes the permanent state, what will remain to become distracted? We will become gadgets.

Are you spending too long in digital distraction? If you feel you are, then it might be time to look at the physical world again and see what you have forgotten how to enjoy or have tried to escape from.

Corporations

The documentary *The Corporation*, explores the idea that a large business is some kind of 'being'. Some of the commentators in the film characterize the being of the corporation as a psychological entity that can show signs of psychosis. A business resembles a human being in other ways. Big businesses can get sick and need recovery time. Like people, they want to thrive. They set goals, have needs, a history and a future, react to stimuli and can experience insecurity against which they employ 'strategies' such as attacking, defending, competing and collaborating.

What role do corporations play in the digital inferno? Big businesses can be very big, and so they can easily pressurize, dominate, bully, threaten, manipulate and create dependency. (Big supermarkets are regularly accused of squeezing suppliers by forcing prices down below their actual costs.) Like a person, a business can be a good citizen too. It can be ethical and benevolent. But the big corporations make decisions according to one criterion: maximization of profit to itself. In that case, they are not like people you would like to meet. Their will is an extension of the will of shareholders who want nothing other than maximum returns on their investment. For such a corporate 'being' to prevail it must have the power to predict and control human behaviour, and eliminate unpredictable behaviour which threatens profit maximization. The corporations need us to be clicking on pages, especially those with advertisements. If we are online 'doing stuff' then advertisers can refine their behavioural models and perfect their targeted advertising.

Lockdown

The corporation needs to get customers to behave in ways that predictably boost the bottom line. It needs to lock customers into predictable and repeatable behaviours. This is where 'lockdown' comes into the market place of mobile technology and social media. The terms and conditions become everything. If you are posting photographs, you sign some of your rights away. You can publish your book on an online publishing platform, but the rights to where that book can later be sold (say, as a printed book) are no longer yours alone. You can have an inbox and a 'homepage' but it must be vanilla coloured. You can't remove adverts from your page (though a wonderful ad-blocking digital revolution has been taking place for years). The platform is designed to appeal to addictive tendencies in order to 'keep you'. You can leave but it will not be easy. You have options within what is tightly prescribed by the corporation. A version of empowerment and creativity, which is dangled in front of users, is really an instrument of the corporation. Freedom becomes defined as the amount of space you have to move around the locked cage. You are free to do as you wish, as long as you stay in the cage. I've even heard this referred to as a kind of 'gentrified slavery'. It is all delivered rather politely and warmly until you question it, or try to leave. This is a business behaving according to its nature. It is listed on the exchange with a share price. Don't knock it — it's a business, isn't it? It needs to control you because unpredictable behaviour is a threat to its survival. It offers you a deal which is becoming more attractive, with cage bars that are appearing to flex and bend a bit, but the deal requires that you stay inside the cage.

Lockdown is usually a voluntary act right at the start. We expose ourselves to it, more or less consciously. If you simply enjoy the benefits of the deal and have no problem with it, then I wish you good luck. Go ahead and enjoy it. If you feel the price is too high, then it's time to find the key to the cage. And here's one way to do it. It involves a shift in perspective in order to see the real extent to which you are possessed by your gadgets. Yes, I mean it. Possessed. Hypnotized. Locked in. Defined, determined and designed. The being of the corporation is now in your head, your heart and your will. It is moving inside you and is even able to overshadow your thoughts, influence your emotional responses and direct your hands and feet. It can turn your usually kind self into someone who is insulting to friends and family. It can make you smile and kiss when you don't really want to. And *it* decides when you will answer the phone and check your inbox. You are left with just enough will of your own to believe that you are the master of your actions but, in reality, you are locked into a predicted set of behaviours from the moment you wake up to the moment you delay sleep to check your *Twitter* stream.

The lockdown looks like this. You can't go an hour without looking at it. Even if you want to stay off it you are unable to for any length of time. You interrupt real tactile interactions in favour of ring tones, alerts and things that really can wait. You have convinced yourself they can't wait. You feel a need to be 'always connected, always on' and you are agitated when you are not. You are spending money on things you don't really need; nearly always, ownership gives less satisfaction than you had in the buying. Your mealtimes, rest times and relaxation times are punctuated with checking up on your gadgets. You hold them in pockets, close to your belly for reassurance. You've become concerned with having enough battery and credit. You always need to be topped up. Your day is increasingly becoming more virtual and less physically real. How is this different to life inside an invisible kind of cage? You now define freedom in terms of this cage, and even if you manage to get out, you will break back in.

On most occasions, when the phone rings, you submit to it and answer. The ringing and the answering are part of a compulsive flow of unnecessary activity that no one really chooses to engage in. Ninety per cent of your online activity is fruitless, 'drawn' out of you by your gadgets and their potential to distract you. Many of us have become locked into automatic and habitual behaviour, checking in, posting, replying, liking and poking. These are now part of life's routine and not to do them makes you a blip in the system. You boast to friends how in control you are when you do switch off for a day but you fooled yourself − like Bilbo in *The Lord of the Rings* when he thinks he has left the Ring on his mantelpiece − by checking your phone three times that same day.

The corporation has you wrapped around its little finger. You've done a deal with the devil and you aren't even sure what the deal was but here you are in the digital inferno. Four members of your family have a mobile phone on a two-year contract. Your five-year-old has become very attached to your tablet computer and two other kids live on their smart phones. You sigh, and check to see if you have any more texts. You checked three minutes ago! You're possessed. Enter the digital exorcist!

Yes, this digital thing is obviously a technological miracle. It can do things which we never dreamed of. But this miracle can also steal your day, dilute your relationships, turn your feelings into simplified smileys and lock you into responding and updating, reacting and posting a whole load of pointless nonsense. What does your instinct tell you? Hopefully, it is to break out of the hypnotic state, unlock the cage and climb out. I'm serious. It could scar you for life trying to get out, or it might be easy, but first you'll have to name it as possession and separate a part of yourself off from the possessed behaviour. You'll have to have an honest look at yourself. It really is possible.

Being your own exorcist

You'll have to distinguish between the 'you' that is watching and the 'you' that is slavishly doing. You'll have to watch your habitual impulses and start to say 'no' to them. You'll have to see the possessed behaviours as *unfree*, and want to move them outside of yourself. You'll have to ensure that actions you take in the digital realm have a purpose and value which *you give to yourself*. These purposeful actions will have a goal beyond killing time and feeling cool using the gadget. Purpose will protect you from the glamour of the machines. You can cease to be a unit in the corporation's advertising revenue calculations. To repossess yourself you'll need to reclaim your will. What do I mean by that?

Try this: deciding when to, and when not to . . .

For a few moments stop reading and just for a few seconds stop your breathing. Then start breathing again. Although we hardly ever make breathing the object of our conscious will, focus upon the fact that you are actually able to do so by deciding when to hold your breath and when to breathe out. Although our body breathes for us, we can also bring breathing into awareness and control it. We can do the same with actions in the digital realm by making them the focus of conscious attention as we just did with our breathing. Who is deciding that we answer the phone? If the hand reaches for it before we even know it, then we are not consciously willing our activity. To undo digital lockdown, we'll have to bring automatic acts of 'submission' into consciousness in order to decide whether or not to perform them.

If you are an addict, then you'll need to make each act of using the gadgets more conscious and considered. You might need help from friends and loved ones. Be patient with yourself, because you'll fail and revert to old ways. If you persevere, you'll gradually find some of the energy that the corporation has stolen coming back and it will get easier.

Choose an hour here or there for a walk in the park without your mobile device. When you feel the urge — the one that is implanted by habit — look at the urge and gently move it away, outside of yourself, saying, 'No, not right now.' You might need to give it up completely, or you might create a routine in which you only use the device at a certain time of day. The key thing is that it is chosen by you as an expression of your will. And then change the routine occasionally. You might be able to love it into leaving you. Don't dramatize it. Just see it as unnecessary, and push it away gently or starve it of attention by ignoring it. The best form of control is to take control of it yourself. Ask yourself: why am I doing this? Is it my choice, really?

Lockdown looks like the corporation is in control and not you. Many people, at a psychological and emotional level, are in thrall to the machine. Confront it. You need to be the one in control. Businesses are supposed to provide a service, but if you are the slave, then who is serving whom? *Slavery* is a strong word but it has been used by those feeling locked into contract terms or feeling controlled by gadgets sold to us with bright and breezy images of empowerment. It is shocking that ordinary people experience themselves as slaves to their computers and unable to leave a social media platform. Perhaps equally worrying are under the radar tie-ins; your content is shared with third parties without your knowledge, your personal details are mined for data without your agreement and you are oddly surprised at how the advertisements are clearly related to things you once looked up for a few minutes.

You must find the conscious will that is truly you. If you do not then the force which possesses you will become you.

Distraction and will

Jan's Diary...

I'm fuming. I was having lunch with an old friend when, after about 20 minutes, she asked me if I didn't think it was rude to keep looking at my phone while we were talking. I told her I certainly hadn't been doing that. Well, not as much as the 'every few minutes' she had suggested. I agreed it would have been rude had I really been doing it that often. I only looked at it a few times, I'm sure. She also suggested it was rude to have the phone on the table in front of me, switched on. She said she saw it light up at least ten times during the hour we met up. When I got home I realized I was fuming, not with her, but with myself. Because I think she was probably right. It's in the pocket from now on. And the ringer will be off. Just on vibrate...

Here is how distraction works. You are at some point in time – let's call it point A – and you've made a decision to do something. For example, you say, 'I will take those gloves back to the shop and change them for the right size.' It is important because they belong to your partner. She asked you to do it while she is at work, and snow is on the way. You decide to do it that day as you are going into town. You put them in your backpack and off you go. On the way you bump into an old friend who invites you for a coffee. You go to a café saying that you only have an hour because you have to get to a shop before it shuts. Time just flies by. Before you know it the café is closing and the glove shop is closed too. You head home with the same gloves you left with. Let's say that point B would have been when your will impulse had been realized and you changed the gloves, and when an objective fact stood in the world in the shape of what had been a subjective impulse.

Now, after your visit to the café, that impulse remains unrealized. Looking back, your will impulse at point A is only real as a memory of an intention. The intention did not become actual. You did not reach B. Point C is when you deviated from a direct line to point B, either by deciding to do so or by drifting along till it was too late. Point D is now the new place at which you are looking back at your unrealized impulse.

Most people get distracted like this and it makes sense to build it into our day as slack. Timing our day down to the last second requires tight time planning and a lot of self-discipline. We can avoid wandering into the place of distraction if we are able to strengthen our will by prioritizing things and holding true to our priorities, but people who become distracted easily find this nigh on impossible. The place of distraction can also be avoided by choosing whether to unite our will with another person's impulse of will, or not. For example, we might have refused to change the gloves for our partner. When we accept responsibility for another person's wish we make it our own wish. We can, of course, just say 'yes' but not internalize it as our own wish and just let the person down.

The success of reaching point B – the point of realization of a will impulse – is influenced by the strength of our will impulse at point A. If we will something strongly, the force of that will impulse helps us carry it through to realization. A strong will impulse contains a kind of golden promise to ourselves. When we agree to do some-thing for another person, we not only make a promise to them to do it, we also make a promise to ourselves to do it as well. How often do we keep those promises and how often do we break them? Sometimes circumstances outside of our control mean we can't keep the promise, but often we break it through distraction. We forget the promise and the result is that we break it. Halfway through that coffee with the friend our original impulse might have been remembered, and conscience awakened in us. *Conscience*, as meant here, helps us remember the promises we made to ourselves and to ourselves on behalf of others. It is the reminder we receive from ourselves if we have broken them. We might feel suddenly guilty that we haven't done what we set out to do. We remember our responsibility and obey an inner voice by telling our friend that we really have to go in a few minutes. 'Let's meet up again,' we say, and then we change the gloves.

So, how strong is your will force and can it carry you as far as your goal? One test of its strength is whether it survives distraction on its way to realization.

Now, let's move our attention to mobile phones and all of that calling, texting and checking-in to status messages on social media platforms. Here, we face the distraction test from minute to minute, especially if we have set it to 'always on' and to vibrate, sound or flash at whatever is coming in. We have exposed any will impulse which is currently working in us to potential distraction from the device. Now, if our will force is strong, and we are on the way to realizing some goal of our own, then it will probably survive a test of distraction. We can ignore the alert and carry on, or briefly look at it and then put it aside. If our will force is weak, then we may allow the distraction to take precedence. Soon we are heading along a path of *un*realization of our will impulse. That simple dynamic can disrupt every moment of our day. We can become disjointed to the point of being like children who pull all of the toys out of the cupboard but never play with anything for very long before looking for another cupboard to pull more out of. We can end up with a huge mess of lost pieces and broken toys.

However, when our tendency to become distracted arouses our conscience then we can get a bit depressed about who we are and at how we often find ourselves running late, leaving things unfinished and vaguely lowering our expectations of ourselves. This can infect families and whole organizations. Distraction and unreliability become regular quirks of character which we come to think are beyond changing. Yes, it can get that bad.

So, often, we might feel that we have failed ourselves when we note that a perfectly realistic will impulse which we had is now unrealized. Our disappointment with ourselves can further weaken the unused muscle of will-power. When we realize we have failed to carry out what we had willed for ourselves it actually makes us feel even weaker. We see the broken promise. This can reach a tipping point at which we surrender to *un*realization and give up. The will impulses of others carry us. We drift along in constant distraction.

Usually the thing which tempts you into distraction is gratifying, pleasurably humorous and stimulating. Somehow, distractions are designed to reach into whatever it was that you were doing and relieve you of its burden. They can do this spectacularly well. Some empty feeling within us gets filled up for the moment by the will impulses of others. We become a bystander who feeds on their superior will. The distracted person can then become the one who relays things made by others. The distracted person passes content onto others and looks for positive feedback that it was 'liked'. So, the person is not only distracted by someone else's content. He is distracted by the role of publicizing someone else's content. Everyone is distracted by everyone else, passing on some cartoon, quotation or link to a cat that sings in tune or looks like Winston Churchill.

While we are all seducing each other down a level by all this, the originators, however, are delighted. Their impulses – their ideas and products – are hawked by willing servants. We become an audience of one that watches life acted out on someone else's stage with someone else's script. When this reaches the point of becoming our real fun in life we have forgotten who we are and have entered a place of wretched contentment. It is wretched because we are now drifting, not fancy free, but determined by forces outside of us. If we were more aware, we wouldn't be happy while being so unhinged from what we originally set out to do.

We reply, we react, we post, we add a friend, we tag a friend, we watch a film clip and we say '*maybe*' to attending some event. Each of these little acts gives us a microscopic sense of being productive – but only while we are doing it. An hour passes and then we look up from the phone, slightly disorientated. Now, what was I supposed to be doing? You had every intention of finishing that chapter. The notebook is lying open at an empty page but then your hand reaches for your phone and you have a picture message. You laugh and you click a link to the rest of the album. You've been tagged in several photos; one you approve of, and you comment. One you don't like and you try to remove the tag, but it isn't straightforward. So you click the 'help' link. This reminds you to check your email about the request you made for technical support with your new camera. You check your email and find the reply about your camera problem. It doesn't really answer your question but instead it offers you a discount on an upgrade to a new camera. You click on the link. There's another email in the inbox that is about a birthday party; you click on that as well. It's from an old friend. You look her up on *Facebook*. It seems she has some 'friends' you used to know. You start to check them out. Another 30 minutes go by. A text comes through and some more emails. There are also some alerts on your *Facebook* page that 'need' attention.

The minutes glide by and you are deep in distraction. There is the possibility that you will order yourself back into line. On the other hand, you can re-prioritize and allow yourself to give yourself up to distractions with a clear conscience. This is one of the natural options. I feel like a break, I am going to check these photos, you say, and find out how to untag, and work on the chapter at four o'clock tomorrow.

By re-prioritizing you can renew your will consciously and make what might have been a distraction into a conscious new beginning. But people rarely do, and their will starts to leak away down the plughole of forgotten intentions. Of course, some people love this formlessness and see it as part of a creative flow, as if creativity was merely the openness to serendipity. It can be good to decide to have a more emergent and spontaneous day, or phase, in your life. So, do it. Make a promise to yourself and stick to that promise. Today I will go with the flow, you can say, but this works less well when it becomes a habit of surrendering to distraction. Mysteriously, it is the free person who is able to stick to commitments.

> **Try this : directing your drift**
>
> Set two time slots aside for 'distraction' stuff. Say, ten in the morning and six at night. Allow, say, an hour for each. During those times you allow yourself to 'drift' digitally, but not outside of those times. For the rest of the day, stick to whatever you have set out to do and if email or text alerts do come through, save them for those dedicated time slots. I'm not proposing that you should do this all of the time. Just see if you can do it for one day.

Soul gym

Realizing impulses of the will in this way is akin to muscle toning. Loss of tone of both will-power and muscle power can be a vicious circle – the less you do, the less you can do. It can also be a virtuous circle – the more you do, the more you want to do and can do. Paying attention to this toning is an investment for when the big decisions come. When they do, you will need to be consistent and strong. They may have to do with achieving something for yourself or perhaps for becoming a person who can support others. Training the will in this way brings inner development to our lives. It makes us better human beings who will look back with a peaceful mind upon a lifetime of intentions which we stood by and took through to point B.

Let's go over this a bit.

I'm at point A. I'm supposed to be finishing this chapter. It's urgent that I do my tax return. I had a letter from Auntie Grace and I want to write her a nice reply. The laptop is out. The resolution is made. Thirty minutes later, it remains unrealized, the coffee is a bit cold, and I have completed 40 tiny tasks on *Facebook* that I hadn't planned to do at all. Most are just responses to stuff put there by people in the hope that someone will respond. I have to leave in 15 minutes. I'll do the letter another time. I order another coffee. The phone lights up. Someone has replied to my jokey comment on that video clip. And someone has retweeted my retweet of a retweet. And somewhere in Canberra Auntie Grace is thinking of me. She strokes the cat on her lap and wonders whether I got the letter she put in the letterbox three weeks ago.

What often goes unnoticed is that when we do reach point B – at which some action is carried through to completion –– we have strengthened something in ourselves as well. Will realization strengthens will, and will is what you need for the big steps in life. Distraction usually weakens the will, little by little, under the radar of our awareness. Digital distraction offers diversions which are undemanding and little by little it erodes our will forces. The problem of social media and mobile phones is that when they become a regular distraction we lose our energy for follow-through in the real world. Soon we find there's an irritated lethargy at the base of the force that we really do need for life. We become someone who can't be relied upon by others, and even by ourselves. We become colonized by the will of others. The real resolutions of the day get traded for 100 smaller automatic responses that require nothing more than reaching for the phone.

Why, we don't even have to get up out of our chair! The place of distraction, point D, becomes an actual place for us to go to. The journey into distraction is shorter than physical world journeys. Distraction can be reached in a second, with minimal physical movement. There's a strong temptation to choose the action that is easiest, so we favour a text over a phone call, and a phone call over a face to face meeting. As lethargy kicks in we find that distraction makes it unnecessary to generate physical energy. And then the circle is closed when we justify unrealization as the consequence of merely coping with distraction and its effects. We forget that at the start, at point A, we had strong will impulses for achieving some-thing; we now tell ourselves that it was not really worth it. So now, instead of a novel we write an occasional blog, and instead of a long letter to Auntie Grace she gets a short email with lots of lazy kisses at the bottom. We once promised to visit her but that is now out of the question.

Mobile technology and social media offer distraction in the form of smaller, less challenging calls upon your will force. You might even feel as if you've been more active by doing many little things online in the time it was going to take you to change those gloves or visit that friend across town. You said 'yes' to changing those gloves. Following through would have taken you from A to B and the golden promise would have made you stronger. But distraction stood in the way and offered you the following brew: *reactivity,* making you the support act for someone else's show; *aimlessness,* taking you along tracks laid down by others, leaving you lost and far from home; *submissiveness,* to a force that is outside of you. Life's vital things just fade away under our noses.

Gadget-binding

Can you walk down a street for ten minutes without reaching for your mobile device? Can you spend an evening without checking to see who has contacted you? If you can't, there is a problem somewhere.

We can re-label inner compulsion as choice. All we have to do is say that addictions are simply ordinary choices which just happen to be repeated over and over. Sadly, renaming something doesn't alter its actual nature. If you like to delude yourself and call your compulsions *choices*, then I imagine you'll find what follows rather irritating.

Those who supply digital equipment claim that their devices are 'neutral', that consumers can choose whether and when to use them and that any problems lie entirely with us. Blame the weakness of the user and not the technology. Well, there's truth in that but also deception. Commercial digital technology is powerful enough for us to become lost in it, and it is designed to increase our need for it.

It is not surprising then that we don't like to be parted from our gadgets. The phones are reassuringly in our pockets and our tablet computers are in our shoulder bag. We have moments of panic when it doesn't seem to be in the right pocket or where we thought we had left it. Our heart misses a beat. We sleep with it by our bed. We twiddle with it furtively in corridors and whilst queuing to pay in shops. We take it to the beach, to church and to all social engagements, at which a visit to the toilet is an opportunity to check in. Not surprisingly, it is simply irresistible to children.

The gadgets promise us a version of psychic connection to thousands of people. We can see with the eyes of satellites, be privy to the thoughts of souls a thousand miles away. The deal is this: one world traded for another. If you feel that trade isn't a fair deal, try some of the exercises mentioned here. The exercises are about knowing what you want and not being distracted by a device that can obscure the real potential of each new moment. One of the biggest dangers of regular digital distraction is its power to erode our ability to will what we really want. We simply get out of the habit of being the originator of our motivation. Reasserting your will can be initially painful and disconcerting but doing so creates a flow which leads to strength in yourself you had no idea you had.

When I was at business school in the 1980s, we were taught the AIDA marketing model, which stands for Awareness, Interest, Desire, Action. The aim of advertising is to create desire through stimulating interest, with the goal of getting us to buy. Advertising is *intended* to drive people towards some kind of compulsive behaviour. We often believe ourselves to have chosen freely when, in fact, we are simply being obedient to a force outside of ourselves. When the invitation is cleverly done — to become a bright and breezy new you complete with shiny new gadget — you will be unaware that you are acting in obedience to the adman.

When compulsive behaviour is extreme it is a form of addictive behaviour. We recognize addiction to alcohol, smoking, gambling, sugar and drugs. Other addictions have become recognized — to television, computer gaming and to social networks, though many find it hard to see these as genuine cases. They see them merely as instances of excessive self-indulgence. This is not the whole story. 'Addicted to *Facebook*' or 'addicted to my mobile phone' might be flippant phrases still but studies of compulsive digital behaviour as true addiction are emerging and therapies will follow.

Just as worrying are those who claim they are in control but are simply unaware of how much they are using their mobile gadgets during a typical day. I've seen people put their phones away after checking for messages only to pull them out again more than 20 times within one hour. I have seen others switch on their phones during meetings without appearing to be aware of it. Such people are like drinkers who have taken many small steps to being alcohol-dependent without knowing it. They break their own rules about not emailing at weekends or after work without acknowledging it to themselves. They feel compelled to be *always on*.

Compulsion and freedom

Perhaps compulsion is just a new norm. It is valid in itself simply because there is no single accepted human norm. It is a new way of being in the digital inferno. Some doubt whether there is anything wrong with having compulsions anyway. As lifestyle choices they are another way to construct one's narrative in the absence of objective norms. Such intellectualism simply covers up an inability to choose self-control and it often justifies this with fashionable dismissal of the reality of the self.

Of course, actively courting the embrace of addictions as a form of defiance – the 'I'll do what I want' stand – is neither new nor is it confined to digital addiction. I have encountered too many who would like to control their digital addiction but say they are unable to. When they try, they inwardly object to the fact that an action – even one they propose to themselves – has any kind of *should* attached to it. *Should* is about tedious obligation, repression and indoctrination. So, it is not cool. It is as if one part of themselves were saying to another part, 'Don't you dare tell *me* what to do.' Or, 'I won't be told what to do,' even when it is one's own self trying to do the telling. This is self-rebellion and it is a kind of illness. When we reach the point of liking the feeling of being run by our gadgets we can see even the judgement of our own self as an authority we need to defy. *Freedom, we say, is doing what we like* and so we feel obliged to do what we like just to prove we are free, especially if there is anything, *even our own self*, proposing that we shouldn't. It's self-respect, innit? But following what we like is not the same as being free or following our inner will. We only think we are free because the liking is a cause of an action which works on us from the inside, but this inner act of liking is itself not necessarily free. This is because we do not necessarily come to like something as a result of a conscious choice. In that case, doing things that we like can be as determined, i.e. unfree, as surely as if we were muscled into doing them by an external power or oppressor. If we insist on doing just what we have come to like, contrary to our inner voice, then we are defying ourselves. We are telling ourselves to 'push off'.

So, here's another invitation to throw this book into the bin. If you do not see your online routines as compulsions, then read no further.

As you are still with me, you perhaps do feel that compulsive behaviour is creeping into your life or the life of someone you care about and you would like to do something about it. There are exercises for you to try out. Most of all I will be proposing that you give your intuition a good listening to. I want you to consider that the deeper intuition *of being you* – I don't mean ideas *about* being you – might be your best means for confronting compulsive behaviour.

The bad news

The bad news is that the wish to be *always on* is a compulsion. There may be times when being in constant touch is really necessary, such as for work or a personal situation. But mostly it is not necessary. People leave home in the morning and their hand is reaching for their mobile device as they walk along the street. It goes back into their pocket as they cross the road (though not always) but then out it comes again. We arrive at the bus stop and 'kill time' by checking what's new on our device, again. We then spend the bus ride to town checking in constantly to various forms of social media. Time flies and we are there. We have noticed no one on the street, been almost killed crossing the road, ignored everyone at the bus stop and seen nothing of the passing scenery. Did we miss anything? Even if we do talk to someone, it is a distracted kind of conversation in the style of 'status messages'. Everything is awesome, 'kewl' and amazing and our eyes flit without resting upon anything. We want our experience to be like a ready meal but reality is all fresh ingredients. Out comes the phone again.

Try this: redirecting your gaze outwards

The next time you leave the house, leave your mobile device in your pocket until you get to your destination. Hold on to the idea that your journeys are not dead, unconnected time. Greet a neighbour and say good morning. Taste the air of the morning, observe the clouds or any of the other ordinary miracles with interest. You can connect to it all, if just for a few minutes. Go on, indulge your physical senses. Breathe in through your nose and smell the air, or get to know a plant's unique scent. Notice any compulsive urge to reach into your pocket. Note the compulsive gesture and with your own will let the compulsion evaporate. You might need to keep on saying 'no' until new interests arise, but keep it calm and gentle. Try this for a week. See if you can last for a week. If you want to go even further, actually hold the phone in your hand but resist the urge to look at it while you are doing this exercise. Observe that compulsive pull to just have a sneak peak. Say a gentle 'no' each time.

This exercise is not about demonizing the digital realm. It's an activity for gaining control over it so that what it offers can be a positive part of your life. Of course, some would say that people are spending more time being 'virtually' connected precisely because of the lack of warm connection with the people next to them. There may be some truth in that but there's still the social and the natural world out there to delight and stimulate us. They both need our unique input. The remedy starts with ourselves. Then, when my phone does ring I can ask myself, do I choose to look at it or is my response conditioned by all of the little rewards it gives me?

When the phone calls on my attention there is for a split second a moment in which I can imagine my self-command or my surrender. It is a moment in which I confront my will. Self-command might seem a stilted and forced thing. Surrender might seem superior, like some flowing state. Surrender, or 'falling into' it, will feel easier because flow states tend to be easier. Yet we can develop a real love of our self-command. We can feel energized and more ourselves when our impulse is ours and not all reaction to external stimulus. We can love the feeling of life's moments being woven together.

Since we do not have the habit of freedom we find that exercising it is uncomfortable. However, strong acts of will are often the gentle ones which emerge quietly from within, and flow sure and true in us like a song. Practising freedom is exercising our will. When we unite our will with our conscience we start wanting to do good in the world. But we lose faith in ourselves when our will is hijacked again and again by distractions. And this can make us lose faith in things in general. Soon, our only act of good citizenship is to pass on funny videos, tag friends in photos and 'like' people's events. On the other hand, each little use of our original will adds to the will force in our lives and feeds the motivation for achieving our goals. This is the secret; we strengthen our autonomy through conscious decisions we approve of and we weaken it by surrendering to inclinations we do not approve of. But it takes practice.

'There can be no river, unless the mountain spring makes a sacred promise to the sea'

Try this: choosing when and if to respond

Each time the phone rings, take a breath and gently take hold of yourself mentally. Saying 'yes' or 'no' to the call will be part of a longer running flow state — one of many points at which you might say 'yes' or 'no'. I may answer it this time, or I may not — neither is from automatic habit. If the phone rings, my slightest movements (of eyes and hand) towards the source of the sound can be, will be, my conscious choice. If you do decide to answer, register this fact to yourself before your physical body begins to act. Act without reacting. Feel yourself winning back a kind of healthy flow state. It can feel like breathing again. The phone rings. Register that it is calling forth a reaction. Be aware that there is the 'thing' and that you yourself are separate and able to ask, 'What am I doing right now and what have I promised myself (or someone else) to do?' Then choose.

The exercises become easier with practice because when we practice we are changing ourselves. The key is separating yourself from the device and its pull on you. Giving up your will to an external stimulus will strengthen conditioned behaviour and weaken your core, little by little. Maintaining responsibility for your choice strengthens you. The spring in the mountains is your own self which appears as if from nowhere, gains in strength and flows out to the sea of your life.

Obviously, the deeper issue here is about the difference between *freedom,* where we are the first cause of some action, and *being determined,* where something other than us is the origin of our actions. We may think we are free just because nothing outside of us is coercing us. However, when we slavishly respond we are not free but are giving up our power to a seemingly benevolent dictatorship which makes us trade freedom for behaving like a gadget. We become a gadget. Our habits become automated and our speech becomes a pre-assembled set of gadget terms. We don't really answer the phone. The phones need us to get themselves answered in order to meet those corporate targets. In terms of Mark Slouka's book *The Assault of Reality*, we become drones in a gigantic hive. We answer the phone because we are in the hive mind.

Trying to achieve freedom in a single bound...

Trying to achieve freedom in a single bound equals failing to achieve freedom. Breaking a bad habit requires regaining resources of will which we gave away in each of the tiny stages by which we got the habit in the first place. When it comes to reforming ourselves we may think that our efforts need to be mighty and our successes grand and reached with a single step. We lose heart when it does not happen like this. But there need be no epic sense of effort and, equally, there need be no unthinking laissez-faire. When the text comes through, a gentle inner act simply measures the value of answering it against sticking to what you are doing.

As we will see later in the book, there are some very simple ways to regain self-control without feeling we are missing out on the digital flow.

The important thing is that you choose to do something, stick to doing it, and do not surrender during that time to digital distraction. Always during these moments, turn the device off. Retaking control of your will with your will can be tiring at first, but then it starts to energize you, and you'll find your will-power increases for other aspects of your life.

Try this: giving your full attention

Take control of where you place your mobile device on your journey. Just for five minutes turn it off. Place it in your bag, not in your pocket or in your hand. Make the conscious choice to be in 'not connected' mode during a coffee break or lunch and make it a priority to connect with the people who are physically there. You might say to yourself, 'These people need my full attention so I will give it fully.' See if you can do it, for their sake as well as for yours. Just to put the compulsion in its place.

Compulsive behaviour tends to strengthen our energy for further compulsive acts and to steal energy from our will-power as a whole. Then there is our conscience. This reminds us that we are neglecting our deeper and better motives. If we ignore that, we drift into listlessness, and our dreams and plans start to float away from us and we come to resent those who have self-discipline. But little acts of will can have a remarkably large effect on our will energy as a whole. We start small.

Try this: gently undoing the digital compulsion

Buy a nice notebook and record a few thoughts or reflections, or plan your day using pen and paper. You might do this on your daily commute. It can be just for ten minutes – which activity is chosen is less important than the fact that in carrying it out you are exerting a will impulse determined by yourself. You might like to take a more careful note of what you see. If it is a regular journey, try to note new things each day and see how rich that picture can become.

See if you can feel when you reach the end of those ten minutes or whatever period it was you decided upon. There is no need to keep checking the time on your phone. Find the time with a best guess. It does not matter if you are short or long. Try it at the same time the next day or even at the same time for a month. The important thing is that you decide. It is your will which decides what and for how long. If you forget, try again. If you succeed in this for a month – at, say, simply choosing a time when to view a text rather than having to react there and then to an alert – your will energy will increase and you will feel stronger inside.

Try this: choose your time

You receive a text. Choose not to respond immediately. Instead, choose a specific time later on to write your reply. Say to yourself, 'I'll reply to that, along with any other texts, after lunch.' Then stick to that commitment.

In all of these activities we are trying to weaken compulsions. The best way is to use digital tools for achieving something which you value and not as ends in themselves. The best way to swim back up to the surface and breathe the free air again is to gently resolve to obey yourself. You might start to realize that you have become addicted to some degree, which would be helpful. But don't make rules out of these exercises. Don't worry if you stumble with them. Gentle resolve and patience will work inside with powerful effects.

Try this: meet the digital tool anew

On a day when you really are immersed in messaging and connecting, try every time you get an alert or message to look first at your device just for a second and remind yourself it is a tool for your use; then decide to read the message then or later. If you do read it, read it and then look away and pause to think over your reply before typing. Don't get lost in the immediacy and the power you get from it. Reclaim your will by choosing consciously the moment of your reply. A few seconds of thinking time away from the screen is all that is needed.

Over the years, living in the relaxed city of Brighton in the UK, I've known more people who cannot refuse alcohol than people who truly choose to drink occasionally. They do not enjoy the drink but have the drink to enjoy. I know almost no one who can choose when to smoke. I know a few people who are on top of their mobile devices and are able to use them mindfully and keep them in their place. I know a lot of people who think they are masters of their digital devices but who are actually very addicted as shown by the way they compulsively reach for them. They miss out on a rich world of people and nature all around them. They are 'connected' while being disconnected from the real world. Whole families are, in Sherry Turkle's term, 'alone, together'.

PART TWO

In Part One I wanted to lay out some general concerns. It may have seemed heavy-handed to casual users of digital equipment. I stand by my analysis of the situation, however. Running through the whole book is my concern that human beings must rise to the challenge which the digital realm presents, and that we do not seem to be doing so.

The next 15 chapters turn to different topics in turn. These topics – such as safety, parenting and computers, chopping life into digital pieces and losing its wholeness – also revisit themes from Part One in different ways.

A point about attempting exercises; it shouldn't be a special effort which interrupts your flow. They are a means for lending will to some of the ideas in order to get them off the page and into life.

2

'Placement' — the Key to Freedom in the Digital Inferno

Placing is what we do when we decide when, where and how we use our smartphones, tablets, laptops, desktops and games consoles. We have control over our lives when we make clear decisions about where and when they are used, how they are used and what for. Basically, *placement* is keeping them in their place.

Often we are lazily reacting to things and end up being driven by the gadgetry rather than being the driver. This can result in poor use of time, or using the device in a less than optimal way. Placement is a conscious wilful act. When I place a process, I claim mastery over its location in time and space, and thus my whole relation to it.

If you are worried that digital devices have got on top of you or your family, placement is a way for you to get back on top of *it*. Getting on top of it is usually a result of skilful placement. Here are four 'placement' choices.

1. *Placement of a physical process in the physical world.* For example, we could place a meeting into some other form — such as an online meeting, a phone call, a virtual chat on a messaging platform, an email exchange — but we decide to locate it in a real meeting room.
2. *Placement of a physical process in the digital realm.* We meet using a video messaging platform such as Skype, or we meet in the virtual world of Second Life.
3. *Placement of a virtual/digital process in the digital realm.* A decision is to be made and we allow a computer to run a program

which repeats some original decision of ours. This already happens when we let a website or service automatically renew itself, taking the money from our bank account unless we expressly cancel it. We might use a program to find the cheapest deal for us for a flight. Even though we will decide whether to book the flight or not, we trust the program to determine the cheapest flights for us to consider.

4. *Placement of a digital process in the physical world.* We could decide to print out a digitally created and stored document onto paper in order to read it in the park. We can, of course, squint away at our screens in direct sunlight but a physical piece of paper does the job better.

The aim of placement is to locate the digital or physical process in a place that maximizes the user's quality of experience. Competent or skilful placement involves outcomes that can be measured in terms of personal, social or business value. Incompetent placement involves placing a physical or digital process in a 'wrong' or 'less effective' place.

Placement can be careful or careless. When it is careless we may find ourselves struggling to make decisions. We may find ourselves in an online teleconference struggling to achieve a sufficient sense for who the other people are. In this case, we really need to make contact in a physical place, in a real face-to-face meeting. This is what Timothy Leary referred to as the 'sacred' meeting, for which no 'virtual' substitute will suffice. When we are sitting in a room trying merely to exchange information that could have been achieved in far less time and with more clarity via a shared digital document or some other collaborative software, then our physical meeting is an example of bad placement. When we are trying to show a new design to others over an online conferencing platform but the colour hues and clarity simply can't be realized online, then it would have been better to have sent hard copy images.

Placement locates human beings, digital device, platform and content in the right balance. It uses the right process and technology for the desired outcome. When we've become digitally addicted, the lazy default to the digital option can lead to sluggish rather than slick communication. It can lead to certain people being less than impressed (often ones who really matter), and sometimes to disaster.

When we are being careful in matters of placement we might hold a monthly team day during which we can develop the necessary rapport for our many online interactions; or we might use a physical meeting because the personal content requires us to be face to face; or we might turn off the phone because the child next to us needs our warmth and attention.

Skilful placement is appropriate to location and time. Part of the measurement of skilful placement is the extent to which resources are saved or wasted. A digital process might maximize effectiveness by reducing the time taken to complete a process, but it might also lead us to miss important details because it passes too quickly. The overall measure of placement is the extent to which it leads to a successful outcome. This applies as much to personal life as to working life. Sometimes grandma needs a physical visit and a phone or video call will not meet the heartfelt need. No amount of typed Xs or emoticon kisses will suffice. Sometimes we need to give other people the time they need to share their worries. Sometimes we need to sit down somewhere private in order to make a shared family decision, and not try to do it on the bus into town. Placement involves seeing the digital options alongside the physical ones. It is about making decisions, big and small, concerning where, when, how, why, with whom and for how long.

Placement involves sleeping on big decisions, switching the phone off during mealtimes and building time flexibility into difficult discussions and challenges. It is quite the opposite of 'just going with the flow' with our default behaviours. Placement is about becoming proactive rather than always reactive. Placement will initially feel less 'kewl' than being blown about the digital inferno. Placement is about re-engaging your will. We can practise some placement, beginning with reclaiming the bedroom.

Kylie's diary

Two weeks ago, in bed, my husband turned to me and said 'goodnight'. I always go to sleep before him and he sits up and reads on his tablet. I said 'goodnight' back, and then, 'Aren't you going to kiss me?' I felt like a petulant teen. But it was the first time since forever that he hadn't. He looked up from his reading, kissed me, and said 'sorry'. Sorry for not kissing me. Something's changed. Something changed in that moment. I feel as if I want to talk to him about it, but it feels like being petty, maybe even paranoid . . .

. . . Well, we did talk about it. Actually, Neil said he was glad I had said something. Two nights later, Neil had a real book in bed, one made of paper! I said goodnight again, and he forgot again! I'd thought it was something about being hypnotized by the screen on his computer but maybe it's more than that. If we are distracted in the moments when we should be aware of each other, then any technology can create that distraction, even the book kind.

Today I'm feeling foolish. I don't need a kiss every night and I don't want it all to become automatic and habitual. It's just that you notice things when they suddenly stop over a long time. Five days in a row now, and a gorgeous kiss every night. And he's holding me, really holding me. The tablet is downstairs and the book has returned.

The devices often sit there, charging up, next to you, in the bedroom, in the living room, by the kettle, in the kitchen. In a family of four there can be four phones with spare chargers hogging plug sockets. Harmless? Convenient? Let's dig deeper.

That little device is filled with the pre-loaded will and pre-set intention of others. The software and hardware designers have built helpful intentions into the devices to facilitate typical patterns of use. But there are other intentions in there too. And get this, they aren't yours or mine. Even when switched off the presence of the phone is a subconscious reminder that we are 'always connected', even in the bedroom. Being connected can serve us well when we need current information. However, at home, in the room where we sleep, how necessary is it to be 'always connected'? I'd suggest that 'always connected' in the bedroom is a symptom of being locked in. Can you do without your mobile phone by your bed, six inches from your head? Could you leave it downstairs or – perish the thought – go from leaving it on standby to switching it off altogether? And, next morning, what comes first, a morning kiss for your partner or checking to see what texts have queued up overnight? First thing in the morning, where should your attention go first? Then, at night, you might just find that closing the door to the bedroom and actually switching everything off is the best preparation for restorative sleep. It might just be the best way of digesting all of that digital daytime flow.

Den's diary

My dad is 82. He got into computers at the ripe old age of 71! He loves his flight simulator and his train simulator, and now he's getting addicted to this hang-gliding game. He phoned me yesterday and told me he was getting worried. He said that at night when he is trying to go to sleep he closes his eyes and can see the moving after-images of the games he has been playing. He also says it makes him feel a bit travel sick. Mum said, 'What do you expect?' Dad is a retired lorry driver. He used to get the same thing when he was younger. He would close his eyes and the road would appear – not very clearly, but just the sense of moving forward, of swerving from left to right, slowing down and speeding up. It used to bother him that his work could have such an effect on him and make it hard for him to go to sleep. Now he's getting a similar feeling from the games. Mum's told him to cut down. I discovered that these computer games (which he can play for a couple of hours at a time) are sometimes the last thing he does before going to bed. He tried an evening where he stopped playing the game in the afternoon. Lo and behold, a better night's sleep and no after-images. It really was that simple. Now he listens to the radio before going to sleep, so now he has juicy night-mares from the news instead.

At night the after-effects of screen images loom before our inner gaze and prevent us from letting go of the day. We are all different and the effect on each of us will vary. Some experience no apparent ill effects, but others find that digital images haunt their inner life. It is well reported that computer gamers see the after-image of games in their inner vision when they try to sleep for the night. They still feel the turbulent *boom boom zap zap* of the gun. In the first days of computer games, when *Pong* was the rage, addicted gamers couldn't get the image of the little moving white dot out of their minds as they lay down for a night's sleep.

Sleep takes up a third of our lives. A good night's sleep is heal-ing and vital to our physical and mental health. There's plenty of evidence that night shift and sporadic shift workers tend to have higher health risks. We've been sleeping in step with the night for a very long time. And when we sleep we process the bad stuff in our souls and harvest the good stuff. We restore, we heal, we dream and we develop ourselves in subconscious ways that make the next day better. In traditional stories and historical accounts, the end of the working day was about putting tools properly away in their boxes and stabling the horses with a calming pat and some fresh straw. It had gesture of closure for the night. We only slept with our sword by our bed when we felt we were in danger. The lullaby and the goodnight story were the gateway into the land of sleep. These, as well as rocking the cradle, dimming the lights, closing the curtains and the soft kiss, are hallmarks of security for us still.

Try this: reflect and review your digital day

At the end of the day, as you prepare for sleep, mentally review the messages you have received. See which ones stand out as significant. Try to picture in your mind the real people who sent them. If you don't know those people, then try to imagine them. See how many messages you can remember without looking. See if you can review them in your memory in reverse order. Many messages are unresolved and disappear quickly into our sub-conscious and as a result our sleep is troubled and irritated. Remembering and reviewing the day, even for just a few minutes, helps you let go of it and put things away properly before you sleep. This exercise helps us to settle, to retain significant reflections and to sleep so that we wake up restored and with clear minds.

Beside our bed might be a cup of hot chocolate, some light reading or some lavender oil. When we turn out the light it is time for a different phase of the day – a time to let go. I'd suggest that being 'always connected' doesn't allow us to let go properly and, at best, provides only the kind of reassurance which the bottle does to the heavy drinker. Turning off the device at night – willing yourself to do so – is a good way of welcoming the land of dreams.

Try this: resetting your inner image landscape

Before you climb into bed take a look out of the window. Breathe in the night air if you can. Look at the sky or the garden. If it is too dark, you can look at a picture, ideally a picture of nature and not something disturbing. Focus your gaze on it for just a few minutes. Don't analyse it. Just let it impress itself upon you. Notice aspects of it calmly, especially the different colours. Notice if any particular colours draw your gaze more than others – the blue of the sea, the yellow of the sunflower. If they do, just rest your attention on those colours and breathe in and out a few times. Then close your eyes and continue to breathe for about a minute, letting the impressions continue to echo within you. Then open your eyes and climb into bed. This little activity can be a wondrous soul cleansing routine which gets you ready for sleep. Have some nice paintings in the bedroom, of different shades. And there's nothing better for this than a real picture, painted with real paint. It can be fun to find one in a charity shop or at an auction.

The digital realm makes it very easy to generate endless images of things which lack the feel of real things. Placing the digital consciously – right times and places – encourages us to counteract that with living rhythms which rely upon us. Placement of our activities over time is always rhythmical. Good rhythms in our life favour long-term well-being in mind and body. A good domestic culture has healthy rhythms, such as the bedtime story for the little people, the walk on a Sunday and the shared meal. When we join successive moments of life with our will it is like the rhythm in a piece of music which joins it up and makes it the piece it is. Proper rhythm makes life whole and it is something on which our living body depends.

Limiting the use of devices as a part of placement isn't an uncool betrayal. Quite the contrary, placing your devices is a conscious affirmation of them; you are putting them in their place, deciding when and how to use them in ways that integrate them with the rest of your day. Reclaim your home by putting your gadgets in the right places and using them at the right times. Is it a fair deal if being always connected to the world out there means that, little by little, our own connection to ourselves and those we love is eroded? Is that a price really worth paying? So, get a little charging station and put it in a hallway or a spare room. At night, plug them all in there. Banish them from meal times, the bedroom and from family relaxation time, not because there is anything evil about them but because they are compelling little boxes. Being always connected means, even if you do get used to it, being always alert, never quite at ease.

Now, let's recap and go further...

Your home is made up of a number of spaces. These spaces do not all need to be the domain of always-connectedness. In fact, 'sacred' spaces are an important aspect of reclaiming your home from the spidery reach of digital connection.

Sleep is actually a special time within the rhythm of our lives. It begins with settling down for the night. And, just in case you didn't get it the first time, if twiddling with the mobile is the last thing we do at night there is a big danger that we take into our sleep the effects of spidery-fingertip activity. It is far healthier to clear the decks before sleep, to spend half an hour without such interruptions. We can listen to the sounds of the night outside, wind down with something beautiful or relaxing, or play back the day in our thoughts gently. Tuning into our breathing and relaxing into our tiredness is a chance to be honest with own bodies – we stop masking the tiredness and are gently taken away by sleep. The quality of our sleep is very important to every other aspect of our lives and we should welcome its velvet embrace.

The bedroom is the first sacred space we should remove the mobile devices from. Charge them in another room. Even putting them away under the bed or in a pocket is an acceptance of their right to be in your sacred sleeping space. Banish them. Place them, like we do with the car. We don't just leave it parked on the street with the engine running. We leave it off, locked and, if there is one, in the garage.

The bedroom is also the place for gently waking up. When we make the transition from sleep into wakefulness we re-find ourselves in a very subtle way. As we are waking up, the sound of birdsong is somehow more refreshing. Lying there, emerging from sleep, we sometimes experience ourselves in a way which is drowned out in the face of the day's demands.

Diary entry November 2010

I decided to kick my phone out of the bedroom. It lasted a couple of days and then seems to have found its way back to its place, charging up, right next to my head, after a short compromise of plugging it in on the other side of the room. I try again. Back it is again and there doesn't seem to be a natural home for it in the spare room or downstairs. Excuses. And the habit of checking it at night and first thing in the morning is too strong. Wishes and not enough of something else. I look at her as she is sleeping. Several nights, the last thing I have seen is not her smile but the messages page on Facebook. She deserves better. Another resolution.

Some people leave the phone outside of the bedroom, charging up in the hallway. The first thing they do in the morning is to check it. Ideally, mobile devices are better checked after three important activities: waking from sleep, washing, and eating. Only then should we pick up the device and check it. Try it and see how it feels. Doing this challenges us to change. We can stumble before we achieve it. If we can make improvements then great benefits can result, such as a happier start to the day with a clearer motivation. We feel more motivated because we value things more correctly, such as valuing our long-term well-being over the fevered pleasures of distraction.

The human being has a need for a genuinely calm transition (i.e. distraction-free) into and out of restorative sleep. The key thing is that a healthy ritual is renewed each morning through will-power.

Try this: delay your habitual digital dash

Leave the mobile outside of your bedroom. In the morning have breakfast or a shower before you even look at it. See if you can wait to look at it for two days in a row. Then three. Then a week. Take a little step and see if you can maintain it. If you falter, don't beat yourself up. Just try again. Do it gently.

Readers of *The Artist's Way* are encouraged, on waking, to write down their freely flowing thoughts to capture their dreams, reflections, worries and fantasies. Meanwhile, of course, the little device will be trying to insinuate itself into your will-power, prompting you to check it before you need to do so, and fulfilling its corporate purposes.

Diary entry March 2012

We've moved into a new home, a three-bedroomed house. The back room on the ground floor is becoming the office room for the house. This will be the place where mobiles are placed. And computers. But we haven't got that room straight yet and it is a bit of a storeroom. The mobile finds its way into the bedroom and the living room becomes ipad and laptop territory. And yet the living room always feels better when it is free of plugged-in things. It is bedtime story time. Why on earth would I ever reach for my phone to see who has retweeted me when a glorious seven-year-old is asking me if Harry Potter is a real person?

Placement acts as an antidote to *always on* addiction. You reclaim your home when you place the device somewhere in particular, so that when the phone rings you must go to it. If you like to walk around while you are on the phone, return it to its place after the call. Such little acts of will reclaim the will-power you lost while you were becoming its servant.

I'd also like to suggest that the kitchen is as important as the bedroom. Eating, preparing food and tasting it involve other life processes that keep us healthy. Some health experts believe we should not even be reading while we are eating. The evidence is mostly anecdotal but their view is that we should really savour our food and allow ourselves to digest it properly. Digestion is important and it happens best when the blood is allowed to flow to the organs of digestion, which is what happens when eating is allowed to be pretty much just eating.

Our will is unconsciously involved in our digestion. We don't consciously will ourselves to digest, just as we don't usually will ourselves to breathe. It takes care of things in the background but we can bring aspects of it into awareness – stop chewing, chew for longer, decide to taste things more consciously. If we swallow too much too quickly we might get indigestion. If we forget our food is there, it will go cold. Eating, like everything else, can be mindless or mindful. As with everything else, digital distraction can make us less mindful of eating. It may seem to be no different to reading a newspaper over breakfast but I'd suggest that we are more distracted when we eat while using an interactive device. We become immersed in digital interaction and zone out of tasting and properly enjoying our food. This might seem no different to eating while chatting with others. Eating while chatting with others at the table just isn't experienced in the same way – at least not by our body – as eating while trying to get a high score playing *Angry Birds*.

When we eat properly and prepare our food with loving attention, it is like being in agreement with our will. Our food does us more good and we get more out of it when we taste it properly. When we cooperate with our digestion it tends to be better for it. Our unconscious will, down there digesting for us, responds favourably to our conscious cooperation such as eating meals calmly and preparing for sleep in some way.

When we are 'always on' we are constantly ingesting content – reading alerts, texts, poking at other people, liking, checking email, downloading, uploading, upgrading, bidding, updating, deleting, opening, submitting responses, hugging and posting. If we do it while we are eating, our multi-tasking is overloading us. As the will attempts to digest the virtual content its forces are diverted from the physical content, our food. It's easy to eat a sandwich in a minute whilst talking on the phone. Some people are skilled at doing both at the same time. Others write a half-hearted, shorthand text while they wolf down their sandwich at the same time. The result can be a misunderstood text with the need for further clarifying texts, and trapped wind. And the beginnings of nervous indigestion. Eat your sandwich. Taste it. Let it go down. Then text.

I confess that it is only in recent years, as part of a family, that I have come to really value the sacredness of the dining table where we sit together to eat our meals. I'm not being old fashioned when I say that the meal table is no place for the spidery-reach of mobile connectedness. I'm being futuristic.

Curtis's diary

I saw someone nearly get killed this morning. He was walking up the street glued to his phone. He looked fairly expert at this as he didn't bump into a single soul though several had to dodge out of his way. He reached the same crossing as me. I looked over at him and saw an alert light up on his phone just as a child said to her mum, 'We can cross now mummy.' The man just went, and the crossing was still set to red. A bus screeched to a halt just in front of the man who looked up with digital oblivion on his face before he realized what a close shave he'd had. He waved an apology then continued on his way, buried again in his phone. I told Sadie about this when I got to work. And she tutted at me, saying, 'Well, you're not much better!' 'What do you mean?' I replied, and she claimed I often did exactly the same thing. Anyway, a week later, we were at work, and Sadie showed me a video she'd taken with her mobile phone. She'd taken it from her window that looks over the car park. It wasn't that clear but there was no doubt who the fool was striding across the car park, reading texts on his smartphone, and dodging dangerously around a car that was just backing out of a parking space . . . Let he who is without sin cast the first phone.

Many people are now willingly trading family time for digital distraction. As families we spend less time together. Many families do not eat together at all. Yet food is the affirmation of life. Food comes from the earth and is one of our many deep connections with it. Distraction breaks that connection. Does that matter? I think it does, because, if we use placement to leave the mobile devices out of our mealtimes – thus fighting distraction – we are affirming a vital connection to the real world with our will. If the meal is with family, we are keeping that healthy family rhythm and connecting with those we love instead of with disembodied presences. The food taste better, and it makes us feel physically and soulfully connected with people in our sacred spaces. We can connect with our food in the same way even when we are eating alone. Placing the device outside of the rhythm of eating puts it in its proper place.

Diary entry November 2012

The last thing I see at night is the smiling face of my love. The mobile phone is next door in the spare bedroom and it has remained there now for a few weeks. The bedroom is now a sacred place for sleep and intimacy. When I wake in the morning I do not rush to check the mobile on my way to the bathroom (as I did in October). The plan is to de-clutter the office downstairs and then that will become the assigned place for being virtually connected. We have no mobiles or devices in the bedroom and none at mealtimes. The ipad and laptop still grace the living room. We just need a decent chair for the desk. We have all the right plugs for a dedicated charging station. That room will be the portal to the digital world, with a lovely view of the garden with double doors than can be opened when it is warm enough. But there'll be no other doors into the digital world from our home. The rest of the house will be ours alone. Meanwhile, I sit in the living room sharing my attention between faceless colleagues in New York and the real but half neglected questions of a curious seven-year-old would-be wizard.

We can start to value the digital realm in the right way when we really do practise placement. We can use our digital devices with purpose. They now have a place – in space and time – and we are investing our will in upholding those places and spaces. We are also valuing the unique potential of those devices, in their proper places.

We start to assign times of the day to checking our emails, so we aren't checking all day. We can look forward to reading the queue of texts. What I am underlining here is that just because the digital realm offers us uninterrupted connection, it doesn't mean that being always online is its prime benefit. Without placement, the effects on our emotional and physical life can leave us ragged.

The benefits of banishing the devices from mealtimes and from bedroom will be different for different people but I can offer some probable general outcomes. You will notice that your productivity and efficiency online actually goes up, not down. You'll notice that you are thinking more clearly when using digital devices. You'll feel less tired at the end of the day. You'll become more able to discern what is necessary and what is empty. You'll find being 'on' a richer experience when it is a choice rather than an addiction.

Saffy's diary

A colleague at work claimed I am addicted to my mobile phone yester-day. I told him he was talking rubbish. He rarely seems to use his and is a bit of a dinosaur. But I don't want anyone to call me an addict. I don't smoke and rarely drink. He claimed someone who needs a drink in the evening is alcohol dependent, while someone who needs a drink in the morning is an alcoholic. He's always spouting made up opinions like that and presenting them as facts. Anyway, I was annoyed and did an online search for the word 'addiction'. It said addiction is the 'continued repetition of a behaviour despite adverse consequences'. Well, I wasn't aware of any adverse consequences. Until yesterday. I received an informal letter of warning from my line manager. It said several people had complained that, despite it being mentioned to me informally on a number of occasions, I was regularly using my phone to send and receive personal texts during work meetings. One person was annoyed that I was looking at photos during his presentation, and another had actually seen me giggle while, to use his words, 'secretly texting to someone on my lap'. My friend Irene, a good friend, told me that during one meeting she saw me checking my phone on my lap about 15 times in half an hour. Apparently the next letter will be a formal warning, on my record. Well, back to the silly definition. Yes, I do feel the need to text in the morning and the evening. Did anyone mention the afternoon as well?

Some people make the home a place for no digital devices at all. Some have even moved to the countryside to get away as much as possible from the radiation and the invisible waves. Others have one room for it. If this all seems like a big leap, then try a few smaller steps. Just try keeping the device out of the bedroom for a couple of weeks – see how that goes. Start with small steps and watch what happens. Placement isn't about dramatic gestures. It begins with a simple, clear gesture that will warm up your will. And once that will is back in your hands your sense of purpose will be your leader.

Diary entry February 2013

I'm using the devices more away from home than ever before. I still lapse and we still haven't properly assigned the back room for being online. But mealtimes and sleep times are now our times. I love our meal times together. I still eat too quickly but not as quickly as I once did. We talk. We laugh. There is no feeling of being pulled away by the gizmos. Sleep is better. Preparing for sleep is lovely. Waking up is lovely.

Now, you may be reading this and saying, 'Yes, it all sounds perfectly reasonable and I want to reclaim my home.' Or you might be thoroughly annoyed at me for spoiling the fun of being 'always on'. You'll sigh wearily and carry on as before. I will counter this with the observation that this occurs when the sense of life is diminished so that there is no longer an appetite for what has been lost. So how do you start at all? Supposing that one has lost the taste for it, how *does* vicious circle become virtuous circle? It can usually only be done in stages and not with dramatic big bang change. If big bang change works for you, that is great. If it doesn't and you run out of steam, then have faith in something within you. It is not a particular thing which you can pull out and inspect. It is a power to grasp our inner activity *with* our inner activity. Take a small step. Then another. That's how it works. The digital realm crept into your life, little by little, under the radar of your awareness. To put it in its place will require little acts of will. Each small step will strengthen your inner will and take you further.

For sure, it is possible to dive into your mobile phone. Soon the virtual realm is all around you. You surrender to it and find you can just let go. In the process of doing so, you gain a sense of ease, but you lose something of yourself, as I will now try to show.

A bright and sunny day...

A text arrives, and you are in the flow. You gave yourself up to the medium years ago, so it isn't you who reaches for the device, but your fingers. It's no different to reaching for another biscuit because your body derives temporary pleasure from it. It is your hand and you let it reach for the phone on your behalf.

So you've picked up the device and it's from your partner and she says she's looking forward to seeing you later in the week. Your finger taps an X and it's gone. An abstraction of a kiss. The real lips do not move a micro-millimetre. It's a kiss without will. When your partner receives the text, she reads the kiss and imagines it and believes it. Well, you do mean it, but not with your will in that moment you sent it. The typing of a kiss was a formula which you acted out. A kiss was imagined by the receiver which had no counterpart in reality.

She replies with two XXs of her own. You read them, noticing them first in your thoughts and then, because there are two, you quiver imperceptibly.

Let us examine this scenario. When we follow certain habits – in the habitual flow – a kind of involuntary will force within our limbs acts without being under the control of our autonomous will. The limbs seem to hold deeply forged memories within them and to 'know' what to do. If we noticed the habit and we've decided it isn't something we want to break, then we let our muscles get on with it. For example, in the act of reaching for the phone – though we might choose to do it and no one is forcing it upon us, it is not necessarily an autonomous self which makes the choice. If what we call our choice expresses inner drives and motives of which we know nothing, then, from that point of view, it is not a free choice but one which is determined by something other than ourselves. Where does our free choice, if we have it at all, come from then? Where is the source of the mountain spring in us?

Another day ...

A text arrives. Your partner has typed, 'I miss you. XXX'
Three kisses! You are doing well today!
A wispy cloud passes over your mind as your fingers reach automatically for the device.
You reconsider and briefly reflect.
You aren't sure why, but in one moment you see your hand as something separate from you, with a life of its own, which is about to type something that you are only partially involved with.
You gave it permission many times in the past to act in just that way. And now, there it is, yours, yet not quite your own.
You flex your fingers as if for the first time and notice the urge to type. You hold it back even though you are still feeling the urge.
You are suddenly stronger for having taken ownership of an automatic urge.
Of course you want to reply, your quick thinking reply is all ready, but you hold back.
And now you are still.
Without knowing why, you close your eyes and try to imagine her.

You are frustrated at not being able to form a good image of her though you saw her only last week and have known her for years.

You exert your will and search for the image – the eyes – not just a diagram of eyes but her eyes, and her forehead, her brown hair, her lips. There are the three kisses.

You remember her kiss, as it flows into your imagination. Now you really feel something in response.

And this feels so much more a part of you than automatically typing a capital X did.

You are separate from it and you can also take hold of it.

And you do. Inwardly you act out that thing which we do when we kiss. It becomes a real inner gesture.

You send it in your mind. You imagine it and you send that to her, across the distance.

Holding that inner gesture which you sent, you now take the phone as if for the first time.

You recall her face and the kiss you just sent from your heart.

Then you type your 'X' and press 'send'.

Some distance away she receives your message with a smile.

One thing I have discovered is that if you slow down your texting, and give yourself time to think about what you want to write and to picture the other person, then, when you press 'send' it feels more conscious and satisfying.

Raf's diary

I always draft my texts. Other people don't usually do that but texts are things you want to say to other people and important texts are important things you want to say. I suppose I am a bit of a letter writer. I still send real postcards to friends when I am abroad. When I text, I always read the text back to myself before I send it and nearly always end up improving it. There's such a lot of scope for misunderstanding in texts. Often I change a word, but sometimes I rewrite the whole text. I like drafting before sending. It's like real writing and I enjoy that. When I get a text I always feel that immediate urge to react and just start typing. But I hold back and read what I've been sent carefully, and then I draft a reply. Sometimes I don't send it immediately. Often I read it again just before I send it and then write something completely different. Often the initial reaction is not right. I see no reason why these little miracles of hand-held technology should lead us to be careless. I'm certainly not . . .

Writing your text as a conscious activity rather than an automatic one, with an image in your mind of the other person, is like tasting food properly. It is the same with reading them. Read it, then sit back and think about it. Reproduce its essential content in your mind. Allow your reactions to sink in *before* you form a reply. Digest it and let it work upon you without staring at some screen which is flashing a million times a second.

We operate in the digital zone all the better when we know we have the ability to leave it for something important. If you love being 'always connected', then good luck. You may love the glamour of cool technology and look forward to cyborg attachments to your nerve endings. You may be an evolutionary prototype, a person who is ahead of your time and for whom being always-on is a new kind of natural.

To the rest of us, I would suggest we all slow down to the speed of our humanity, and enjoy its pace when deciding where to put our feet.

3

Staying Awake, Keeping Conscious at the Computer Table

The next exercise is for avoiding going off on tangents, sometimes called WILFing, which stands for 'what was I looking for?' It stands for the mental confusion which takes over after we have been wandering, clicking on links and passively reacting to what is in front of us. This happens when our will goes to sleep and we drift about looking at all the enticing things like a child taken to the fair for the first time. To oppose this, at the end of a period of computer use we can review our activities and ask ourselves whether we had a particular goal for that session. How close was it to our intentions? We can review what we did, in reverse order and in pictures rather than in words, from the last actions to the first ones. The last thing was … before that it was … before that … and so on back to the first action we took after the computer was up and running.

Try this: staying awake in the digital inferno

Here's an exercise for protecting your sanity which you can do during the annoying two to three minutes your computer is booting up.

Imagine your intentions for this particular session at your computer. What do you intend to do and how long will you spend doing it? Decide. Commit to your decisions. Look away from the computer when you are doing this, close your eyes if it suits you. *Just don't stare at the start-up screen.* You can be specific about what you are planning to do this session: send some tweets, respond to an email, etc. And you can choose more open-ended activities, such as some web research into travel to France. Now, in your mind, allocate time to the tasks. (Write it down as a list if you want.) We envision our intended actions forwards in time, and use the computer boot-up time to consciously orient ourselves towards the time ahead.

The first part of the exercise is a ritual for strengthening conscious intention; the second part is a healthy closing of the process. It reduces the danger of our will activity dwindling to being a mere function of the passing allure of what is dumped in front of us. We can go to sleep in a very subtle way when we use a computer. We become a function of digitally delivered material until our inner activity becomes fainter and finally dies away. If we catch ourselves 'WILFing' we can correct our approach and resolve to stay more awake next time. It's an honest look back, comparing what we actually ended up doing with what we had intended to do. The ideal of course is that we did what we intended to do.

Simply put: make a plan when the thing powers up, and reflect on what you did when it powers down. If there was a WILFing gap, resolve to reduce the gap next time round.

When we close a door with a 'Do Not Disturb' sign we are taking time to focus on a task. We are doing the same when we switch to silent or work offline. And just as there are devices to time-lock you out of the refrigerator, you can also set your computer to prevent you from going online for a while!

Try this: digital working without distraction

The next time you write your emails, use a word processor and not the email programme. You can paste them in afterwards. Enjoy focusing on the task of writing. Ensure all other programmes that could distract you online are switched off. Close your browser. Focus on the task and see it through to completion. The key challenge here is to work without digital distraction, so you will need to switch any other devices off.

Of course multi-tasking is great but sometimes we need to give full attention to something. We do that in physical life and there is no good reason for allowing our concentration to be regularly distracted by the swirl of the digital inferno. Having the ability to focus and resist distraction at will is a fundamental tool for life. You might find that you can't concentrate for very long. That can be a tough realization. An inability to see something through is a sign that distraction has begun to take control of you. Reclaiming focus will make it easier for you to see things through, offline as well as online.

Common sense is going to be a necessary starting point for anyone who wants to remain awake and alert in the digital realm. For example, if you must spend hours with laptop on your lap, at least put it on a supporting laptop stand and be careful your pillow or cushion doesn't overheat in case it catches fire. Who knows if fertility will be compromised from the radiation so close to our reproductive organs? Even if there is only a faint possibility of that – and at this stage science is unable to rule it out – are you prepared to take the risk? Locating laptops and desktops on computer tables with upright chairs and supports for your back and wrists helps to place them properly in space. You have to go to them to use them. Using them becomes a bit more of a conscious decision so that your will is involved a little more each time you power up.

Try this: being upright and properly poised for the digital realm

Sit in an upright chair at the computer desk. Complete a task while sitting with your back straight. Be aware of any hunching over or neck craning. Being upright is conducive to being alert, aware and ready. Perhaps you've got into bad habits. There's still time to save your spine in old age! For any hour spent at the computer, take a five minute walk outside. Even a few moments spent going to open a window, look out and breathing in some fresh air can be of value. Find an object, such as a cloud, a tree, a garden – ideally something from nature – and look at it as if for the first time. Take it in. Then go back to what you were doing. Digital connection of any kind is an immersive experience. We tend to zone into it and zone out of our physical surroundings. Every hour, climb out and touch base with physical reality.

We know a lot about the danger of too much screen time. There are standards for how much time we should be staring at a screen before taking a break. We know that bright screens need to be dimmed and that our concentration can diminish if we use a computer for too long. It is shocking to see how, in our personal lives, such rules are rarely observed and common sense goes out of the window. Crumpling yourself over a computer will play havoc with your neck and back. Staring at a bright screen from three inches will damage your eyes. And over-immersion of all kinds in the digital inferno will have damaging consequences for your body, mind and spirit. So, get up, break the spell, recover yourself by being the one who truly decides what, when, where, why and how.

Zone in to reality through your senses. Re-enter with your sense of smell. Get up after an hour at the computer, go into the kitchen and put your nose up to something interesting. Rediscover what a strawberry smells like all on its own. Kick-start your sense of smell before you head back into that odourless realm. Smell a plant. Try to refine your powers of observation. Go beyond the initial smell of 'it's a strawberry'. This is what we do when the senses are on automatic and just serving up data to our concepts. Go for the subtle elements which make the thing what it is. Or you might say to yourself, 'It's a strawberry but it is not a great strawberry ... maybe because it was picked green on the other side other world...'

Re-engage with your sense of taste. Go to the kitchen and find some little something to taste. Again, it might be a piece of fruit. Roll it over all parts of your mouth and tongue. Go beyond the general impression and, as in wine tasting, see if you can find the different components of its taste. You might close your eyes while doing it. If you don't have time for that, then reach for your coffee and taste it as if for the first time. Give your attention to what happens in your taste buds for a few seconds before returning to the tasteless realm.

Re-engage with your sense of touch. A stress ball is good for this. But get up, walk around and find something to grasp with the whole of your hand, not just your fingertips. Try something like a piece of wood or an apple or a stone. Feel its uniqueness. Close your eyes and see how much you can tell about it without looking.

Your feet can also go out and play. Take off your shoes. Head out onto some grass and make contact with the ground. You can 'ground yourself'. If you can't go outside, just do it in the room. Before heading back into the gravity-less realm focus on how you are planted into the earth down through your feet, and how you grow upright to the sky through your spine, neck and head.

There is you, there is the computer and there is some hybrid monster called the 'you-in-the-computer'. If your work and play keep you too long in the digital realm, you will fall in. If you want to remain conscious, then paying attention to your senses is one of your best ways. They need only take a minute. The benefits are great and the investment in time is small. See what works for you.

4

Gaining Mastery Over the Mobile Phone

An old friend introduced me (back in the early 1990s) to the concepts of 'tool', 'prosthesis' and 'cyborg' in relation to hand-held devices such as mobile phones. Those who are uneasy with the feeling that the phone is becoming an extension of the hand will see these concepts as being prophetic.

In researching for this book, I studied pictures of 'craft' workers from the Middle Ages, the time of the guilds, when most artefacts were made by craftsmen. Many paintings and etchings show the craftsman and craftswoman sitting at a work bench or table, leaning forward over the work. One can detect the control as well as the separation between the worker and the tool. There was a vital separation between the worker and the tool at the start and at the end of the work.

Apprentices were taught the importance of what I have been calling *placement*. Here it refers to the importance of placement of each tool. It is set down deliberately in its proper place, picked up and held properly, with appreciation and attention. Placement was fundamental to the work. At the end of the work day, tools were cleaned and placed back in their rightful places, on shelves, on hooks, in cupboards. The images really do show that detachment between tool user and tool. Separation brought a necessary detachment that impacted on the craft worker's skills. At some point, a skilled craftsman might experience 'oneness' with the tool and go into 'the zone' feeling the tool so completely as if it were an extension of his arm or hand. It became more of a 'prosthetic' thing. The worker might say to himself, 'My chisel becomes part of me,' or, 'My paintbrush lengthens my fingers.' The oneness of the tool user and tool was the crafting just as we ourselves might experience that the dance, the dancer and the dancing are inseparable aspects of the same thing.

The flow state of craft work, where all attention is in and with the work, was a unification of actor and script, singer and song, writer and word, sculptor and clay. The tool being used – the pen, knife, hammer or needle – was the conduit for this flow. So when we engage with content and achieve that flow state called 'being in the zone', then the subject and object can unite. Pictures of crafts folk often give us the feeling that they are in communion with their work. There is calmness within this kind of attention, even when the image is of a blacksmith crashing a hammer down onto red hot metal.

At the end of the work, sitting back, cleaning up and placing the tool back in its proper place re-established the separation, so that the worker could leave the process and *get out* of the 'prosthetic zone' of oneness with the tool, and back to the state in which he had arrived, detached from the tool. Coming 'back to themselves' was critical to being properly 'in the zone' at all.

I am trying, with this simplified picture, to point to the importance of separation from the tool before and after going into the 'prosthetic zone'. Many modern crafts folk say that the 'before and after' separation from the tool has a tangible impact on the quality of their work when they are actually 'in the zone', and that this applies also to the quality of their family and social life. You have probably felt the lingering effect of a hat worn too long on your head or of the images of a computer screen replaying in your head after hours of use. Detachment from too much attachment brings us back to ourselves and we re-cover ourselves within our original skin.

When we get used to them, prosthetics can begin to feel part of us though they do not simulate the lost limb at a fundamental feeling level. Our imagination linked to our physical experience can start to normalize them into feeling part of us. A paintbrush, when I am in the zone, can feel like part of my hand. In the virtual world *Second Life*, where you can create and inhabit an avatar version of yourself that can walk and fly, some wheelchair bound people have reported that it has been so convincing that they genuinely feel as if they can walk and fly. They feel as if they've miraculously climbed out of their wheelchairs, if only for fleeting moments. And of course, many others have reported no such experiences.

The notion of the *cyborg* applies when the tool itself becomes so attached to a limb that we not only direct our skill and energy through it and start to feel it as part of us but we also receive its feedback into our nervous system. The 'cyborg' is a two-way, looped prosthetic device. It is a part of us and influences us actively and dynamically. I'm holding a mobile phone and it vibrates, telling me I have a text. When the phone vibrates, in my hand or against my thigh through the lining of my pocket, then I vibrate too. I've even heard someone who has just received a text say, 'Excuse me, I'm vibrating!'

Often we experience our physical tools as if they are prosthetic devices, but with digital technologies we can go further and imagine them to be part of us. Current technological innovation is aimed at turning those imaginations into physical reality. We are already piloting chips inserted under the skin and wires stimulating parts of our bodies. The futurists say that brain implants are only just around the corner. Soon we'll have augmented reality glasses with information projected onto a screen in front of our eyes with zoom-in capacity. It won't be long before that becomes a brain or an eye implant. On the back of developments in limb replacement in health care, we'll soon have stronger legs, better eyes and ears and cleverer brains. Somewhere up ahead, around the corner, science fiction will become real.

So, we have a tool we are working on as a subject works upon an object; we have prosthesis which gives us an imagined replacement or extension of a limb; and we have a 'cyborg' which is a prosthesis integrated with our body, improving and even game-changing our abilities and potential. I believe that mobile phones are usually tools, often prosthetic devices, and that smartphones are rapidly showing signs of developing into cyborg extensions of our limb and nervous systems. At the very least, there is a preparation for future 'cyborging' of humans going on here.

The more habitual our phone use is, the less separation there is and the closer we are to becoming, or acting as if we want to become, cyborgs. A necessary separation that craftsmen once saw as essential to their work is lost when we keep our phones under our pillows, beside the bed, in our pockets, vibrating against our legs and acting as extensions to our senses (with camera and recording functions). The beautiful creations of the crafts process reflect unity between tool user, tool and material. There is being 'in the zone' but also separation. *The beautiful creations exist only because the creativity arises from somewhere. The separation of the craft worker from the tool emphasizes the fact that the source of creativity is in the self.*

Placement requires a similar distinction between ourselves and our digital devices. It prioritizes the effort to imagine some purpose for using the device. But when separation is inadequate, with the hand poised waiting to pick up the phone, it is as if the phone were an actual part of the hand.

Try this: leaning into the digital realm

When the phone rings or vibrates, do what the crafts person used to do at the start of work. Sit up deliberately or lean forward. Reach forward so you are leaning over your phone and then pick it up and use it. Here you take hold of it with a clear separation between you and the tool. Try it. You become the user of the tool, fully separate, and the phone becomes the tool. Then at the end, look at it as a separate tool and place it back on the table before sitting back.

Becoming less reactive and more decisive re-establishes yourself as the user and the phone as the tool. It can even make you consider more consciously whether you need to answer the call there and then. I'd also propose that it will improve your conversation and writing for calls and texts.

If the phone is in your pocket when it vibrates or rings then, as you go to use it, become aware of your separation from it. This need only be a moment. And before you put it away, register it in your mind as a thing, as your phone. Even better, keep it in your bag so you have to take it out and put it back. Create a clearly chosen place for it. Such placement is always an act of the will. It is your gesture for establishing a distinction between you and the device. You come back to yourself when you do this. You reassert who is master.

We can become immersed in the zone when using our devices. We can be so in there that we are oblivious to our surroundings as we carry on a one-sided shouting match on a crowded bus or nearly get hit by a car while crossing the road. Digital immersion seems to blur the subject-object relationship. We can become an object while our actual inner self evaporates into thin air. We can become tools of the digital inferno and less awake to the task of being ourselves when we are on crowded buses, in streets, and everywhere else.

Separation is just about the only way I know for staying awake and aware in the digital realm. We hold our own when we separate 'I am' from 'I am this'.

5

Speaking on the Phone

I was on the train watching a woman speaking into her mobile. She was the loudest and most animated person in our carriage. Everyone could hear. She was unaware of how her fellow passengers viewed her. It appeared to me that she was the least aware person in the carriage. She was playing a part and had no idea that she was. Her artificial tone and her words were strings of clichés, a style acquired perhaps from certain television programmes. I concluded that she had this type of conversation a lot. Perhaps this is how it is for her every day, I thought. When she stopped the call, she looked drained and a bit like a zombie. She checked her phone at least a dozen times during the next hour. Maybe she was waiting on an important call, but I have seen the same thing too often for that to always be the explanation. So I wrote this book to try to help.

The following exercise is for keeping in mind the fact that behind the disembodied voice in your phone is *that* unique person to whom you are speaking.

Try this: evoking the image of the real person

When answering the phone to someone you know, take a moment to picture the face of the person, either while the phone is ringing or in the moments of greeting. Just hold the image there briefly before you begin the conversation. If it is a long call try to reconnect occasionally with that image. The aim is to remain aware of the actual person to whom you are actually speaking.

Our awareness of the reality of the other human soul becomes dull when we speak merely to a disembodied voice or consider merely its abstract content. It's a downside to instant connection. It is only partially addressed by grainy video calling. Picturing the person requires another little act of will and keeps you a little more awake during the conversation. At the end, pause, and recall the image of the person you have been speaking to once again. When next you see that person you can bring the image to mind again and see how accurate it was. A variation on this is to imagine more aspects of the person, such as the mannerisms.

It can also help you to remain anchored in reality if you tell each other where you are. 'I'm sitting in a noisy café surrounded by garish wallpaper,' or 'I'm on a crowded train.' Including such physical descriptions in a call strengthens our hold on physical reality. This returns voices to their bodies in their physical locations.

Now, let me appear to contradict myself with a different exercise.

Try this: listening to the other person deeply

In this exercise we don't call up an image of the other person at all. Here we try to enter with attention into the quality of the other person's voice. Listen to their voice as they are speaking and simply enjoy the quality of it. Listen for its warmth, movement and unique qualities of intonation.

In that exercise we can enter into the voice with interest and let its characteristic tone work upon us. The idea is to move beyond just content and allow the quality to work upon you. It is another kind of content. In looking for the meaning of the sound picture of someone's voice, you make some effort to attend not just to words but also to the person who speaks them. You meet the other more deeply when imagination is a will activity which reaches out to things. Suddenly, listening to someone becomes a creative, active process as well as a receptive one.

This exercise will probably lead you to focus on your own voice in a new way. How do I sound in relation to the other person? Is my voice different to how it is in other conversations? Does it reveal anything about my inner state and attitudes?

You might find the quality of the other person's voice calls forth inner impressions which are impossible to describe. While you are feeling those impressions you are also trying to capture the meaning of the content. It can require will-power to listen in different ways at the same time. I believe that one of the real secrets of staying awake – and not going on automatic pilot – when using phones involves being able to register conceptual meaning as well as nuances of feeling. This enables us to take in content and also to experience the human being behind the content. If we *give* our listening to others we can better understand what they mean. This isn't a matter of a one-off submission to some rule but an attitude for sustaining throughout the call.

We might have to slow down a bit until we are more fluent in this deeper kind of engagement. If we can be led by our slower part we will gradually develop more lively ideas, respond more richly and have a fuller range to play with. Those who talk (and type) too quickly when using digital media commit their ideas and responses way before their slower, deeper understanding gets a look-in. In this way, dry intellect and cold feelings too often win out. We might be meant to find something impressive in cold intelligence, as if it gives the one true version of reality. This is an error we all seem to be in. The result is that we lose our wholeness.

By allowing both the words and the deeper impressions to work upon us – a bit like how we listen to music – we come to see the whole human being in a new way.

6

Digital Dancing in Short Sentences and Sound-bites

Tweeting and other forms of microblogging involve writing messages comprising a limited number of characters. With *Twitter* the limit is 140 characters. I'll be referring to *tweeting* in this chapter as an example of many different kinds of micro-blogging. Tweets can also be shared across different social messaging platforms at the same time, such as *Twitter, Facebook*, and *LinkedIn*. *Yammer* is another microblogging platform which is used inside businesses and organizations.

Much of our social communication is now in short sentences (updates, tweets, status messages, comments), pictures and short videos. We can share very large pieces of work in the digital inferno but the usual daily sharing through texting, tweeting, status updating and photos – all stuff we love to be distracted by – is delivered in small bits.

Tweeting is the quintessential form of this. We share news, ideas, announcements, links, challenges, rants, stories and humour in 140 characters or less. The trend is towards shorter is better. The assumption is that we need to get our contribution out there as quickly as possible and if it is shorter it is more likely to be looked at, understood, liked and shared. Perhaps it is that in the digital inferno we have short attention spans.

Sometimes the swirl is like the twister in *The Wizard of Oz*. We are at the centre, looking out at things tearing around us at great speed. Timelines grow by the second, discussion threads lengthen and news changes constantly. To stay in touch we need to receive alerts and train our wits to keep our bit as short as possible. Shorter can be sweeter, like those traditional Japanese poems called haiku which have three lines and 17 syllables. A brief form like the haiku is demanding and it takes practice. As with the tweet, it isn't easy to capture the essence. There are various tools for cramming that essential meaning in. There is the same cut-down *textspeak* used in phone messaging, as in 'I L U' for 'I love you', or 'RT' for 'retweet', which means that you are passing on something by someone else. The shared web links look like a secret code.

Tweets are often posted 'on the go' using thumbs and fingers on phones. Fingertip typing is limiting. There's something pokey, sharp, intellectual and not very warm blooded about fingertip communication, like a spider in its web. You can learn to type at lightning speed while taking too little time to find words for things you really want to say.

Here are a few good habits for microblogging, if you want to stay warm blooded and not skim over the virtual web on automatic, like a spider.

Try this: stop bumping into street lamps

Try this for a week. When out and about, do not tweet while walking. Tweeting and walking is like driving and texting. People have got very good at this kind of multi-tasking but it releases agitation within us, whether we notice this or not. When you walk, walk. When you tweet, tweet. Stop, sit down and *then* write to your heart's content. Even if you have to stop a lot, you'll feel the benefits. And instead of tweeting on the go you might meet some fellow members of the human race while out walking. They can actually inspire you to write in a positive way.

If you can tweet sitting upright and at a slower pace you will bring a healthy poise to your tweeting. A decent chair helps. Uprightness isn't just physical, it's a natural sign of being aware and awake. A slower speed is more efficient in the long run. It will allow wisdom and warmth to enter your thoughts.

From my experience of the communication styles in use in online chat rooms I would say that most of it was cold, clever and technical. When I met people face to face whom I knew from chat rooms they were usually warmer than their digital versions. When online, they tended to be warmer if they were sharing something of themselves, such as their stories and poetry. However, the atmosphere of the chat room had looming over it the possibility that intellectual fights would break out at any time. In fact, they did so every few minutes. People who had never met insulted each other. I even witnessed death threats. Of course there was warmth aplenty too, but if you take a look at some comment threads on *YouTube* you will see how people can allow some part of themselves off the leash to attack complete strangers. (And what part of us are we letting off the leash when we do so, just because there is no consequence?)

I'll be describing 'chat rage' later on but here's the nub of it. When our will is disconnected from our heart (and possibly from our better self) and becomes a direct channel for reaction then we can become impulsive in the wrong way. Such impulsive acts can become chains of automatic reactions flowing through our fingertips at lightning speed. How it all feels, to oneself or to others, doesn't get a look in until we pause, if we pause, that is. Yet, it is in the pauses that we perceive the after-image of what we have just let loose upon others. We might regret the argument that exploded after a few quick text messages to our partner, or wish we hadn't sent that one line email to a colleague in which we committed ourselves to something we might not be able to deliver. This kind of thing is going on throughout the digital realm. It is partly why I call it the digital inferno, because we are blown about by it. What slings and arrows of outrageous fortune, when our sincere offerings provoke derision and even hate! You may have witnessed something similar in comedy clubs, when audiences drive a new comedian off the stage. It has never been easier to derive mean-spirited satisfaction from being inhuman as now in the digital inferno. In the digital realm there are many who give free rein to their anger and chat rage can explode out of nowhere. People who have never committed road rage or hurled abuse at a comedian feel empowered by anonymity, their own and their victim's.

The quick response can also be unintentionally insensitive and easily misunderstood. Being aware of what one really has in mind to say becomes even more important when interactions are short, fast and automatic. Does the medium itself tend to eat away at our better social self? It seems that way, though we can counter it with awareness.

Try this: hearing your own digital voice

Always read your tweets aloud before you press the 'send' button. This brings your tweeting back home, rather than coming out of some abstract word processor inside your head. Hearing them brings them to an awareness that your automated fingertips do not possess. It might be a bit awkward at first. If you persevere you might find your tweeting becomes more original. Inevitably, if you edit your tweets a bit you end up with better tweets. You may frown less too!

And when we write in automatic mode, too often the muscle memory in our fingers reaches for the cliché.

Try this: the pen is mightier than the tap

Get a paper notebook and put it next to your device. Write a first draft of your tweets down by hand before you type them. Writing with a pen makes use of the 'whole body' of your hand. You will find it is slower but that the slower process helps to bring previously underused, subtle aspects of yourself up to the surface, with the result that your words really will begin to say more fully what you mean. It can be surprisingly refreshing to make yourself think ahead in the way you need to do when you are writing with a pen.

This diary entry is not about tweets but about writing in general, keypad versus pen.

Tania's diary...

It's been a bit of a revelation, and a painful one at that, to realize that my creative writing has got worse. I've been attending the group once a week and, at first, I thought the tutor was nuts when he said that my writing might be more clichéd and repetitive because I was writing too fast on a keyboard. Actually I sometimes use my phone. I challenged this and he suggested we try an experiment. He asked me to write 500 words on an agreed topic and bring it to the class the following week. I can write easily. I wrote 500 words on the morning of the class on my laptop in the café. He sat down with me and pointed to several clichés – and I had to admit they were there – and pointed out where I had repeated myself. He then asked me to write another 500 words on a different topic, stipulating that I use pen and paper. He even gave me the pen. It was a good one, the kind which went over the paper smoothly. Once again, I wrote my 500 words on the morning of the class. It took three times as long, and I had to cross things out. I also noticed a bit of neck ache from leaning over the paper. I usually slouch backwards with my phone or laptop on my lap. I took it in to the class. Without doubt, there were fewer clichés in there. And no repetition. The tutor said my writing felt fresher – less slick, more genuine. He said it had more promise than what I'd offered the previous week. I'm not sure if I agree. I don't like the idea that I might have to write three times more slowly. But we'll see...

Efficiency gains from using digital technologies may lead to losing complexity and depth, spontaneity and open-ended freedom. Don't trade speed for that richness. Pause, remain aware and prevent yourself from going on automatic pilot – and from missing the real drama that is all around.

Try this: the power of the pause in the digital drama

After a few minutes of tweeting, stop and take a few deep breaths. Step outside. Observe nature. Look into the sky and watch the clouds. Nature is a wonderful place to 'come home' to, especially after working on a computer or a mobile device. The benefits of fresh air are well attested to, while squinting at the mobile or staring into a bright screen has never been doctor's orders! Open a window. Breathe fresh air and be still for a moment. Give yourself a bit of recovery time. Try it between tweets. See what happens.

There is a flow between your tweets which is, or can be, important to you. Tweeting *can* become more creative and meaningful if we look for that flow. Some tweets do stand alone but others may be part of something which is developing in your own mind, or between you and others. Your tweets can be important. They go into the world and cause ripples in other minds. Giving them reflection time will also help you notice and keep track of what is really going on inside of you.

Try this: tweet review

Look back over your most recent tweets, ideally in reverse order. Go back over them looking for the themes that run through them. Reflection is a really useful thing for us. It can unclutter us. How might you have written that tweet differently? You will be surprised how differently you will read them when you see them anew. How did that string of replies develop? Oh! I did not really mean to say it like that! Oh, that one makes me laugh again! Look back over what you wrote and what the others wrote. Look and pause, reflect and pause. Harvest all of those observations you have made, about others and about what is working away inside of you. It can help us to make wiser choices in the future. Reflection helps us to 'file away' our actions and organize them into a kind of library. They go inside, get forgotten and then come out again as a kind of wisdom. Reflection does not happen when we only react. In that case, we don't harvest our experiences, so what we end up doing is like trying to plant in the same ground, over and over. Reflection enables one to see one's evolving story. Like any story, ours can have direction and coherence or not, depending on how mindfully we write it.

I have noticed that tweets written by people who think about the unfolding narrative of their tweets tend to attract more followers and re-tweets. People love a good one-liner but they also love to see stories, ideas and successive tweets which develop something.

Try this: the backwards tweet

I'm serious. Try to tweet backwards. It will be hard. It will feel awkward and unsettling but it is hugely awakening. It brings you right back to making meaningful language. It is brain gym for tweeting. You start at the end of your 140 characters and go back to the beginning. Whenever you feel you have gone too far on auto-pilot, have a go at some micro-blogging backwards.

I'd like to set a challenging proposition before you, especially if you are a regular user of *Twitter* and other micro-blogging platforms.

I am rather saddened by the narrow use of *Twitter*, where those who post try to cleverly cram information into a limited number of characters.

That is certainly one use of micro-blogging, but by no means is it the only use of a once ground-breaking way for people to share knowledge.

Words are an infinite resource for expressing myself in ways that are not just functionally clever, but also eloquent, poetic and inspiring.

The challenge to express yourself in 140 characters opens up possibilities first explored in poetic forms such as the haiku.

Less can be more, and the beauty of language can be realized and enjoyed not through cheap trick shorthand, but through skilful simplicity.

Words can dance, embody rhythm, they can erupt with passion, become a heartfelt call to action, a plea for response, and can carry laughter.

A lot of tweeting misses this opportunity, and I believe people have fallen into a habit of being shorthand-junkies, trapped in their heads.

Microblogging can and should be more eloquently beautiful, more poetic, reaching for the kind of 'dialogue' described so well by David Bohm.[*]

We have an opportunity to commune, not just communicate, with an immediacy and simplicity that could add inspiration to all the information!

Go on – try tweeting a bit without all the neat abbreviations, acronyms and shortened links. You will be surprised at the power of language.

Enjoy a bit of wordplay! Oh, and by the way, every paragraph in this passionate little post is exactly one hundred and forty characters long.

Recently, during the Edinburgh Festival, while editing an online theatre publication with over 8000 followers on *Twitter* I did some analysis of tweets. The well written tweets used complete words and had at least 100 more responses than tweets with cool shorthand and shortened links in them. Interesting, innit?

---

[*] Bohm (1917–1992) suggested a method that allowed for equal status and 'free space' in communication, and the appreciation of differing personal beliefs.

Try this: the physical can deepen the digital

Sit back from your typing and do something physical and tactile. Look at your hand. Close each finger slowly into a fist. Let your fingers unfold until your hand is open. Stand up. Stretch your hands up to the ceiling and take a deep breath. Every so often, break away from your intense interaction with the machine. It also takes will to *stop* doing something you are right into, especially when you really need to in order to free up your body and come back to yourself. Close your eyes and feel the weight of your feet on the floor or your bottom on the chair – put your attention there, even if only for a moment. This is a way of 'remembering' yourself – a way of putting your body back on. When we are tweeting and typing, our attention falls away from our body and flows in a direct line between a part of our brain and our movements on the keypad. Take time to reclaim all of what you are when you are away from the machine.

If you try these exercises you'll be amazed at how much more creative your tweeting can become. See your tweets as a form of art. Then they will be. Bring colour into it. If you are about to tweet something exciting, write it in red first! If you are in a particular mood, splash the colour of your mood around a bit, and then tweet.

7

Following Through in the Digital Inferno: The Case of *Facebook* Non-commitment

Last year, I was involved in running an event in Brighton, UK, called *The Critical Incident*. We marketed through the Brighton Fringe Festival. We created paper posters and flyers, tweeted and made *LinkedIn* and *Facebook* event pages. On the *Facebook* page, over 150 people said they were coming – not maybes, definitely coming. Eight people showed up. Thankfully, we also got about 140 people from that other source called the real world. They came via posters, leaflets and face-to-face conversations.

It led me to wondering what '*Facebook* commitment' is all about. I've experienced this phenomenon before, not just on *Facebook*. I've sometimes put out a text about an event to a number of friends and colleagues. I get replies such as 'see you there!' and 'can't wait', only for those people not to show up. Is it my aftershave?

Social media-based commitment is a very different creature from 'physical world' commitment, though there are overlaps. But the sheer magnitude of no-shows for *The Critical Incident* deserved special mention.

Lisa's diary

We wasted a lot of food. I'm sure people had good excuses and I intend to find out what they were. Fifty-one people said they were coming to the party, and there were 44 maybes. Well, maybes, that's fair enough. But over 50 said 'coming'. Twenty-four showed up. Even some of those 'looking forward to it' didn't show. At first I felt rejected. Then I felt let down. Now I'm wondering whether people just lie outright because it is on Facebook. *Perhaps what you type isn't the same as what you might say when you look someone in the eye. I wonder if it would have been any different if people had said they were coming over the phone? Well, that's the last party invite I'm ever doing on* Facebook.

Why do people say they are coming? Some people *always* say they are coming to my events and *never* do! I think part of the reason is the unhinged and detached nature of the medium. It is usually the fingertips or thumbs that physically commit but not the rest of the body. Fingertip commitment is light. It has a light touch and a light connection to the will, especially to resolutions that need to be realized later in time.

Fingertip commitment leads to promises that are imaginary ones. It is a kind of daydream. It is not a commitment to action but only to intention. Commitments to intention are often transitory, momentary, and they weaken over time to the point of being simply forgotten. They have little or no weight in three dimensions. I wonder what would happen if the 'Yes, I'm coming' button was only activated by human voice. Would that change the probability of commitment to intention becoming a commitment to action? Commitment to action is more lasting in the memory. It reaches beyond fingertips and down into our feet, getting us up and walking, firing our restlessness.

Often we want the other person's or group's event to be a success and we know they are advertising it publicly. As a friend or loyal colleague we say we are coming, in order for it to look as if the event is gaining in popularity. We lie out of a good motive; but we lie nonetheless. Here commitment to intention is a kind of 'thumbs up' to the intention of the other person, a way of saying 'I'm committed to your idea, even if I am not physically committing to anything.' Commitment to action may not come into play at all.

Another factor is a bit more worrying and it relates to what I call *false revelation.* It's a kind of collusion with our own mediocrity where the act of committing to intention *habitually* replaces the commitment to action. We lie to ourselves, convincing ourselves we have really committed because we have said so. I wonder if this would be different if there were an option, say on *Facebook* events, to report who actually showed up to the event? What if there were a naming and shaming button? I've mostly given up with using social media for promoting events, although *LinkedIn* events seem to have a little bit more commitment to action about them if *The Critical Incident* is anything to go by.

It would be better if commitment to intention were replaced by a 'support' function so that people can like an event or give it a thumbs-up. They can openly ally themselves without lying! But the combination of the factors mentioned above is bringing the reliability of social media based events pages into disrepute. I have some anecdotal evidence that easy commitment to intention is beginning to reduce the usefulness of social media in the workplace, making it harder to coordinate meetings.

And yet a virtue is also to be found in all this. *Facebook* commitment is somehow liberating as well. Commitment to intention is a form of imagination and positive thinking. But this aspect of it is hard to indicate. Events pages need better design so that people are able to show support for an event, for its ideology and values, without being forced to say whether they are coming or not. If you are worried that you are someone who has started to commit in this way and you'd like to get back to a firmer kind of commitment, then it might just be time to step up.

Try this: make every response utterly truthful

If you receive an invitation to any kind of event over the next few weeks — a party, a meeting, someone's theatre show — make your usual reply via social media, email, text, or however. If the reply is a 'yes', then make sure it is a real 'yes'. And just to make it a real one, use a more confirming method of communication. Phone and commit by voice. Try to see the people face to face, where you can look them in the eye and say 'I'll be there'. The reason for doing this is to add weight to your commitment, to bolster your will force. It helps the pendulum swing back towards making good on commitments.

In the digital realm we can fly quickly from place to place. But this kind of flying can make us flighty. Fingertips are not the same as a firm, committed handshake, and a ticked 'yes' box isn't the same as looking someone in the eye and saying 'I'll be there.'

A close friend of mine, the founder of a school here in the UK, gave me the privilege of recording her autobiography. She had spent a lifetime inspiring others and setting up projects all over the place. Even in her early nineties she had a crystal clear mind. At one of the recording sessions she asked me what I thought was the root cause of most of the world's problems? After I had made a few guesses, she pointed her long, never-texted-in-its-life right forefinger at me and answered: 'The little white lies!'

8

Losing the Thread

Someone posts a video clip on *Facebook*. Someone writes a blog post or starts a discussion thread. A few people reply. Then along comes someone who makes a bigoted remark, or tries to be provocative, or is just plain misunderstood by someone.

'You a**hole!' 'You ignorant sh**!' Several replies later the discussion has descended into all out verbal war and exchange of expletives. This is chat rage, or the digital equivalent of road rage, when complete strangers are suddenly hurling abuse and issuing death threats at each other over nothing. When it's anonymous, nasty and threatening it is called trolling, and people can get hurt. Especially youngsters. It is mostly just verbal fisticuffs. Your kids will stumble upon it regularly, and they'll find it under the cutest of cat videos.

I carried out an experiment this week on a range of content sharing platforms – *YouTube* and *Facebook* among them, and several news platforms which allow unmoderated commenting or where the moderation lags in time behind the actual posting. In nine out of ten cases the most recent comments were salvos in a war of words between posters who had, I suspect, never met and in most cases were not even 'on topic'. Not a lot of clear thinking was on display, only mean-spiritedness needing to go somewhere. Of course, much of it was entirely unsuitable for the eyes of children.

Interestingly, the layout of nearly all discussion threads which operate without a moderator shows the most recent posts first. One then scrolls down, often needing to click on links to earlier pages, manually, page by page, until one finds the more considered, original comments. This means that the original point of the thread is more or less out of sight. It amazes me that the structure of threaded commenting in social media hasn't changed so as to avoid this problem.

Tagging and automated moderation mostly do not work. Even where content is aggregated and 'hot topic' posts are collected (such as leaderboards on the community social network *Ning* for the most popular posts and posters), it is automated and the result is primitive. It is based on counting up how many times someone has posted, or how many replies a particular thread has. So, if someone is abusive ten times in a row, or if a bunch of people correct the spelling of someone's name, their comments hit the top ten as 'hot content'. Then, if threads are mostly abuse and undisciplined argument, and the wrong posts receive prominence, new comments will not relate to the ones which were 'on topic', and clarity is lost. Replies related to the topic can disappear into history, many clicks away. Later comments then become threads in their own right, detached from the initial point. On rare occasions, comment threads do evolve and build upon each other and open up interesting and novel lines of exploration or discussion. Too often, they are mud fights and death threats. Perhaps it is time for designers of micro-blogging platforms to come up with something better.

Most online communities are lightly policed or moderated, if at all. Most of these platforms are free or low cost, so who is going to resource it? We cannot usually moderate each other's comments in a discussion thread, so more super-users who can police threads are needed. In fact, I see no substitute for wise, community-minded moderators tending chat room threads, like gardeners pulling out the noxious weeds. Without better moderation, whether by computer programs or humans, it seems that the hopes we placed in 'Wikis' and crowd wisdom fall flat. ('Wiki' stands for 'what I know is', and it refers to the content arising from the wisdom of the many rather than content which is formally, hierarchically controlled and edited; the best example is probably *Wikipedia*, an online, crowd-created encyclopaedia.) Too much nasty chat rage flies beneath the 'abuse' radar and flourishes right under the watchful eye of 'intelligent' machines which succeed in merely blocking a few swear words. It sends poison into the world, and to what end? This is the digital inferno in which we exercise the popular idea of freedom. This is the worldwide reaction against censorship and Victorian stuffiness! Get real! So, even if the original offering was fascinating, heart-warming, enlightening, surprising and constructive, often the resulting comment flow shows what happens when we peel off a thin layer of civil restraint – the worst kind of 'free' speech releases more human pain in the digital inferno, and that releases more pain, which releases more...

Try this: look out for thread danger

Before you forward a link to a piece of content that your kids might see – a video clip, a cartoon, an image, a joke – check out the responses to it and make sure the responses will not give them nightmares or leave them with pointless, crude and sordid images to deal with.

Recent news stories on the topic of evolution nearly all have comment threads in which creationists trade crude insults with Darwinists. It is nigh on impossible to find intelligent and considered replies hidden among 200 or so angry retorts. Where it goes really wrong is when later comments which are detached from the original posting spark bar room brawls. A potentially intelligent thread is lost and so is the considerable potential of the platform. Losing the thread is indeed a regular occurrence, leaving us with Chinese Whispers – the original point is forgotten and people react to reactions. It is hard to understand why anyone would see the medium, if used this way, as an outlet for their intelligence.

Try this: chase the thread to its source

The next time you respond with a comment in any part of the digital realm, try to read the entire thread of comments. Where that is too large, seek out the original post and comments and respond to that. Don't get drawn into the distorted, off-topic banter. This will help to set a good example for others.

One of the biggest problems of constant exposure to abuse and rage is that we lose our ability to have a full range of feelings. Exaggerated positives cut this way too; digital praise uses a superlative where 'good' in the real world suffices. This also distorts our judgement. In the inflated semantic currency of the digital realm we need more and more abuse, intensity, violence, as well as compliments, until more again gives practically nothing at all. The same desensitization occurs when we use virtual violence and general ghoulishness as entertainment. Numbness sets the tone of our lives. The news is a Hollywood drama but less entertaining because the special effects aren't very good. Pink Floyd described the condition as being 'comfortably numb'.

Chat rage, or *Comment rage syndrome*, deserves further study. What is it that causes strangers to fall so quickly into hurling accusations and abuse at each other? I think the answer resembles what we know of road rage. Not everyone is good at multitasking, and those who are not tend to slip into cold behaviour, as a default, when they are under duress. For some, driving is a technical and demanding activity, so driving and being social at the same time is hard for them. So when someone else causes them to slam on their brakes, they pitch into immediate irritation and fight-or-flight adrenalin bubbles up. Similarly, when someone reads an original post and the reply to it, he may find it easier to respond to the one which prompts the most immediate reaction. Such reactions will be, of course, less likely to be conscious and free.

Try this: mindful posting, commenting and responding

Be more mindful and selective with your posting, commenting and responding. Respond to what seems to be essential, and not to what is most recent, entertaining or shocking, or to what seems to demand a reaction purely for the sake of a reaction. Try to go back to the original idea.

A daughter of a friend posted her first cover song on a video-sharing platform. It wasn't a bad effort. She was devastated by some of the hateful comments she received from complete strangers. Should she toughen up? Is that the best way for her to feel her way towards her creative future?

The realm of social interaction and content sharing on the web is an ever-expanding garden with noxious weeds as well as flowers. It will be so much better if we all head for the blooms, not the weeds.

9

Looking at Pixelated Images:
A Deal with a Devil?

I am aware that the following might make me seem like some grump wedded to the past. I'm going to risk that.

I am going to propose that computerized images and painted images are removed from the *live* experience of looking into, say, a flower or a human face in a way we need to take account of, and that computerized images are even further removed from their original source than those painted by human hands, and indeed that their essential technical nature employs a kind of deception which our vision fails to detect. I am mostly focusing on the fact that pixels and oil paint are powerfully different, not one better than the other, and that those differences have consequences for the way we see ourselves. So, look away now if you will be irritated to hear that pixel pictures are essentially illusions. Keep reading if you feel this to be true and would like to work with those illusions in a healthy, self-aware way.

We can forget that atoms are not really little red and blue balls joined together with minuscule matchsticks. The little solar system model of the atom is only a theoretical model of whatever is really there. That line of questioning seeks answers to do with fundamentals, the micro-level, the bottom of things … if there is one. At the level of ordinary everyday objects like trees and people we meet with emergent properties. No oil or watercolour painting can be reduced to tiny balls or little jigsaw pieces, or fundamental electromagnetic forces. At least, an *explanation* of the painting is not to be found through reducing it in that way. Its explanation, if it has one, is in the way it emerged as a unique and whole form, as a result of human creativity. When you plunge your brush into a pot of green acrylic and dash it onto a canvas you make a form which makes the world slightly different to what it was before. There is no splash which emerges quite like yours does. The quality of your particular quality will be unique. It will elude any quantitative description of it. This is not so with even a billion pixels even if they appear to be the same as paint to our physical eyes. This isn't intended as a moral judgement, though there is a moral to it, deep down. It is just the way it is. Pixelation is a *rendering* of reality, painting a creation of it.

Interestingly, there is nothing you can do about it even if you wanted to. Paint is always infinite in its flowing variability. Pixelation is always a finite number of discrete pixels. When looking at a painting we are looking at a kind of infinity. Even if our senses are fooled on the surface by a copied picture, I believe we have a deeper experience that 'knows' the difference in quality between the finite and the infinite. Philosophers have battled down the ages about the nature of the 'thing in itself' that is 'really out there' beyond our own selves, and about whether the essence of things eludes us or not. Perhaps that deeper 'knowing' is really an affinity between our own essence and the essences flowing around us but behind ordinary self-conscious awareness. As one or two of those philosophers would have said, 'How else does our knowledge of things get from *out there* to *in here*, in me?'

However, when looking at a picture rendered in pixels, we see the finite and any sense of infinity is illusory. By now we should have dropped attempts to trick the senses by reproducing physical images. We are either being kidded along or else kidding ourselves. It's a shame really. Of course we can store images and share them quickly. But beholding them is purely a sensual thing. It's as much about where we are sitting and where the picture is, even with whom we are sharing the experience.

This is not *down on* digital art. That is a new art form in its own right, original and imaginative on its own terms in the medium of the digital realm. Digital art is worth looking at and enjoying. I wish more of it were available to the general public. Instead, we keep trying to dump physical reality into copied, digital forms.

Try this: gaze for a minute before clicking

The next time you see something you'd really like to capture on camera, before you take out your digital camera or smartphone, just look.

Look for about a minute. Take it all in with your own senses. Then take out your camera. See if you can decide – at least roughly – what shot you want to take, before you look through the digital viewfinder. Then use the device. Aim the camera. Take a picture, perhaps a few. If you can, let the image you capture be largely decided by what you were seeing when you originally looked, not by what you are seeing now through the viewfinder.

You might be surprised at the pictures you take. Less really can be more if we avoid just snapping in the moment. The pixelated image will then capture not only what is there, but also aspects of our relation to what is there. The picture becomes a record not only of the scene before us, but also of our involvement in that process. You'll even be able to tell people later, who are looking at and perhaps admiring your photograph, what your feelings and intentions were. Of course, we can do this looking through the viewfinder, but the act of looking at the miniaturized, digital image of what is in front of us, the little pixelated rendition of reality, can limit what we really think is before us. Our eyes have formed over millions of years of evolution to work with light. You can talk about primitive receptor cells all you like but how this actually occurred just is a mystery. 'The eye is formed by the light, for the light,' said Goethe. So, try it. Let the real light be your guide. It is what made your eye, according to Goethe. Look first. Then take up the device and let it serve your view. Click less, and less might just be more.

One way of staying conscious when looking at pixelated images is to remain aware of what they are. These pictures may be beautiful, may look utterly real, may make us laugh or cry, and they can have enormous value as artistic expressions and digital 'captures' of reality, but they are, at their core, finite. They have quality, but not the 'quality' of creations of infinite possibility. When I look at a pixelated photograph I encounter a simplification that has exchanged infinity for the finite. It is a creation of finite possibility.

A painting of a field of poppies is not only one step removed from the original, it is also a new reality in its own right. It is a kind of species of one. A pixelated photograph of the same field is also removed and also has unique qualities, but it is not a species of one; each pixel is a generic building block. It is modular, like a part of a jigsaw puzzle, replicable in its entirety and at heart unoriginal. It is unable to transform the infinite possibility that lies there, waiting to emerge. It is a kind of simplified record of what is there, a summary, a gloriously complex spreadsheet. But there are no spaces in between the ones and zeros, indeed no space for mystery.

Digital images arise from elements added together from the outside. When adding parts to other parts in the finite realm, no matter how complex the additions are, we no longer enter the realm of mystery, for there is nothing between the one and the zero, the on and the off, the dots or the squares, not even empty spaces. This finite realm is based upon discrete digital steps. This realm has a known bottom level to it – we know this because we made it. Not so the real world, most of which cannot be understood through being reduced to separate, finite units in the way that any machine can be. The real world does not seem to arise from layers or particles being added on from the outside. Certainly living things do not. These emerge as if they were an expression of some law which governs them from within.

Programs, however, can be added to and made more complex till the image on a display screen fools the senses into having a per-ception of a 'reality' which is like another world, one so similar to our own that it hardly matters. It is a virtual — an *as-if-real* — world. Why split hairs over the difference? Well it matters if the differences between the infinite and multiples of finite things are all and everything to what and who we are.

Try this: imagining freshness and the first moment of creativity

When you look at a computerized picture, look away for a moment, perhaps close your eyes, and with your will work your way into what you feel and think the picture might look like if it had just been painted, the paint still wet on the canvas. Doing this is using a certain kind of imagination. Imagine the spaces in between that the digital picture cannot capture, even at the microscopic level, such as a wisp of colour, a slip of the brush, or the stain of the artist's sweat. Then look back, enjoy both images, value them both for what they are, but do not confuse their essential truth with each other.

The real thing is a kind of mystery, and this next exercise is a kind of contemplation of that idea.

Try this: remembering the unique quality of the real

Look at a digitized photo. Then turn away and look at something real, perhaps the sky or your hand. Say this to yourself: *this hand cannot be resolved to ones and zeros. There's something essentially different about it which goes down into something living which is joined with my own being.* That photo is a suggestive illusion. I can enjoy it for what it is, but I shouldn't confuse it with the infinite possibility of what I see when looking at my hand. Pixelation creates a model, a rendition of what is there. Pixelated images can be indistinguishable from physical reality to the naked eye and yet the spaces in between, the nuance and subtlety can be lost, simplified. The smell of paint still fresh on a canvas, and knowing that a picture is an original, can make a profound difference to our relation to it. Would you go to the Louvre to see only copies up on the walls?

Of course, copying is happening more and more in the digital realm. Children are painting one picture at Christmas and the same picture is then copied digitally and sent to all the relatives. This can be a lovely gesture, but I guarantee that a relative will usually still ask: 'Did you paint this yourself?' When the answer comes, 'Yes, but it's a copy,' then it is somehow less than, 'Yes, and it's just for you.' The digital realm is home to easy copying, rendering, airbrushing, modifying and enhancing. These are all potentially wonderful innovations because of the creative possibilities they permit. Yet, if we lose the ability to value originality over copies, we also lose the ability to be original. Here you have a choice, one which has stirred debate for over a hundred years. It has to do with the idea that 'there is nothing new under the sun'. For many, all that the digital realm has technologized is a self-evident truth – everything is a copy. There is no originality. The copy, when it deceives the senses is as good as the original, because the original work of art was probably a copy of something else anyway – so what does it matter? Human beings are 'samey' according to this viewpoint. We are not, each of us, a unique species of one. Originality has little or no value any more because it is a false ideal. We overlap, we emulate each other, and we copy all the time. The skill is how to copy more successfully than others.

Nevertheless, I've encountered much originality in the worlds of art, social science and industry. I have witnessed 'wow' moments and a thousand sharp intakes of breath across a packed room when live music, poetry, drama and storytelling light up the souls of those present. I've stood before paintings for an hour and been drawn in, affected and changed. I've witnessed countless others having equivalent experiences, and how their different responses all go towards making the multi-faceted meaning of that music or drama or painting. Part of what made these experiences so affecting was that the creations were unique, live and real, in this world. I've sought out reports of similar experiences in the digital realm. They are there, especially when the digital work of art is unique and innovative, ground-breaking, hugely funny or shocking. In all these cases, the impulse of artistic creation is aimed at originality. Even when pre-existing images are combined, the impulse can always be towards an original assembly of elements, images, sounds and words.

I have found more people, even among the digital 'natives', who prefer nature to digital versions of it, who prefer original artistic work over digital copies. This extends even to a preference for printing off a letter to read, rather than reading it on a digital device. (Of course, all of our reading may become digitally based if 'digital paper' takes over. That process began when the printing press replaced the scribe. Yet there is still something important about a person's unique signature and a painting someone did just for us.)

Pixelation offers a lot of benefits. It can bring detailed images of real things and of things which are remote from anything real onto our devices and right into our living rooms. Yet the quality of the physically present original image needs to be venerated. It contains its originator's willed gesture within it. When we stand before a painting by Matisse we have that gesture before us in the painting. When we make a digital image of the painting, even an exact copy, the digital image and the forces of creation become detached from each other. When we see a copy it is an echo of something else and we don't relate to it in the same way. (I can say 'I love you' to a parrot and hear it echoed right back to me, but I would be crazy to ... well, it's obvious, isn't it?) This is why original art costs more than copied art. It is why people go to galleries and grandma's face lights up when she asks, 'Did you paint this yourself, just for me?' and the child's answer is, 'Yes!'

This is an old-fashioned view. Perhaps it is so fundamental that rediscovering it makes it a progressive one. Digitized art creates all kinds of possibilities. We can take it so far that we forget the uplifting, sometimes breathtaking impact of the original source. Sadly, children who have only been exposed to digital images of nature can be challenged by the experience of a real forest. Even nature can disappoint when we have become used to synthesized images of forests which show things which cannot be seen in a real forest. Yet after spending a few hours in the forest, we awaken once again to nuance, subtlety, scents and sounds, unpredictability and infinite complexity. Real nature presents us with the vitality of the infinite flow, even within the shape of a pine cone. There are no pixels with empty spaces between them.

Try this: turn your attention to the line between real and virtual

If you've been looking at pictures on a computer for some time, go out and take a 15-minute walk. Stop here and there and look for a minute or two at a leaf, a cloud in the sky, or even the paint marking a parking space. Just look, observe and let the image impress itself upon you. And be aware it isn't made up of a million dots. It is different. Just different.

The next exercise proves that all this is not down on the digital.

Try this: go visit a digital art gallery

Seek out some digital art online. Some will be static pictures, some animated, based on sound and film, some may even be interactive. It may draw on material from the real world, it might be more abstract and generated with purely digital processes. Step away from the world of digital copying and find and enjoy some original digital art. See how wonderful and creative it can be without the need to simply ape the physical.

Digital art is a fairly young art form. It can be compelling, inspiring, even life-changing. Clearly, digital pictures are not 'bad'.

Their technical wizardry can be as breathtaking as a master painter's when he makes stunning copies of original paintings. Digital art employs its technologies and processes to transform ideas, visions and impulses to create something new within the digital realm itself. It goes far beyond the gimmick of pixelating the physical. But the building blocks, we should never forget, are finite ones. The digital pixel is a static little building block, like a child's building block with an extra function; it can be altered electronically. We can get hold of it, to render, manipulate and recreate.

As the technology develops, the increasing number of pixels on our screens might fool us more and more by coming closer to infinity; and some will claim that it actually does. The complexity will be so great that infinity may no longer matter – unless we remain aware. This awareness will hold on to the possibility, at least, that infinity is transcendent; that it is not a distance or a period of time and not the extension of some sequence of units. It is where the human soul lives. If we give that up we will become very confused about what we are.

This is why I am concerned by excessive immersion in digital images. We upload our 1000 holiday images. We watch film after film of landscape and scenery taken from every possible angle, sharpened, filtered, airbrushed, enhanced, edited for the exciting bits, reordered and re-coloured. What about our experience of the real thing while we were there? Perhaps it is too demanding, somehow. It has become too demanding for the child addicted to TV and games who, on being taken on a trip to the Yellowstone National Park, turns to his parents after ten minutes and complains, 'This place really sucks! There ain't nothin' happenin' here!' 'Er, well, no, it doesn't suck. Quite the opposite, it spurts, coz every 90 minutes that water comes up with some force and it ain't some gizmo down there saying it's time!' And such imperviousness to wonder is the tip of a very disturbing iceberg.

On the day I've been writing this chapter I've been reading about teenagers of 13 and 14 (and there is an increasing number of them who are as young as six or seven) who regularly look at pornography on social media sites which are policed by robotic programs with ineffective filtering. There is a lot of sexual violence and bestiality to choose from and our young are in there visiting just about every legal and illegal gallery of images on earth. And Generation Y is creating its own labels and language to describe these images, and turning back to the real world with hard tastes for which mutually caring sensuality is too subtle. Our abilities to self-limit and self-discipline often don't kick-in until our mid-twenties, but meanwhile such images have been lighting up the biological 'reward centres' in the brains of boys for years. They then bring these expectations to their real-world girlfriends. The digital realm, in this respect, is teaching brutality to the young. Scare mongering? No, the evidence is in.

Once, in the past, only the wealthy had access to images, and even that amounted to the few paintings and sculptures in their possession. Most people had hardly any access to images of anything much at all, outside of the church. The effect, when they did see them, was profound. Exposure to the endless succession of images we experience daily can create image overload and lessen their impact. Actually, I think it is more than *can lessen;* it probably *does lessen* and does create overload but we are all so blasted with low quality images that it is hard know what it feels like without them. Peaceful, probably.

We can become so used to this image megaflow that we stop looking with everything that we have. We have to. Another way of saying this is that our soul's imaginative reach into real things is less and we see them with what Goethe called 'a gaze that stops at the eyes'.

10

Talking to Yourself

A few days ago I was walking through area called the Lanes in my home town of Brighton. A man was walking on the other side of the road and talking to himself. It was an animated conversation and so he drew looks from passers-by. We are more used to seeing people with disturbed behaviour like that on the street. Then we notice other people walking along, yakking away on Bluetooth headsets, and it looks the same. This man wasn't using a headset though. He was actually talking to himself. He seemed articulate and angry into the bargain. He was causing some discomfort to people around him and they avoided him.

People talk to themselves for very different reasons. It can be mental illness, or something else. Many people, including some who are perfectly well put together, confess that they talk to themselves. You'll find published scientists, pop stars and actors all admitting to speaking to themselves out loud. But, for most, it's a bit 'freaky'.

So, was the man walking along the street talking to himself 'dotty', or was he perfectly sane and just being different? In this particular case, I think he was a bit disturbed. I also had the impression that he didn't have anyone else to talk to. I felt a bit annoyed at myself and at the other passers-by because we just . . . passed by. I've seen him since, on a bus, and there he was, having an argument with himself again. Some children were pointing and giggling at him. I wondered again whether he simply has no one else to talk to for days and days and days.

As the digital inferno sweeps through our lives we are witnessing people at first hand who look and sound like they are talking to themselves. Of course, they are usually talking to someone else, but that someone else is also somewhere else! Holding a smartphone indicates this though even that does not lessen our disquiet when a man is stomping along the street shouting at someone at the other end of a phone line, heedless of the path he is clearing through those coming the other way. The digital realm extends our field of communication beyond the space that we share with others. During our call, our voice or bodily gestures cannot be interpreted by others around us, just as the conversation cannot be perceived by them. Someone can be staring at me and not realize it as he concentrates on calling some unseen person at the other end a 'jerk'. One day, when we are kitted out with augmented reality glasses (and other technologies that project digital content into our field of vision) our physical and digital realms will overlap more and more. We will all be doing it together!

This will make us more connected, but connected to what? Is being more cut off from our present space and social situation being *more connected*? Being more connected digitally will mean that walking along the street, driving or travelling on public transport will become opportunities to 'check in' digitally. However well this fills the 'dead time' of travelling, there is nevertheless the loss of contact with the world around us, in the present moment, right here, right now. We exchange the unfolding fresh moments in real life for digital connection. Sometimes the trade might be worth it. It won't be worth it if we can't help disengaging and 'zoning out' as we walk along the street. And *not being able to help it* is a distinct possibility.

I find, living as I do in a western culture, that the vast majority of human souls avoid having more than split-second eye contact with strangers. We are 'alone together' in the street, in cafés, in public places. Sure, that suits a lot of people very well indeed. But what if you seek contact and conversation with others? What if the distances between us don't suit you? Contact became more difficult when it became risky or eccentric to start up a conversation with a stranger! It still happens at music festivals, storm-hit bus stops and wherever a bit of human empathy is still OK. People greet others when they are out walking their dogs early in the morning, especially their fellow dog owners. Pursue that further and they get anxious.

Mostly, ours is a culture of mutual avoidance. Not surprisingly, we get the buzz of necessary connection with others from the mobile device. Communication is with a select few at a distance. It is so easy and so accessible. There's no eye contact or physical touch. The digital realm will get you connected within seconds, and you can even pretend to be someone else. We might see this as a wonderful new thing – a chance to connect to a whole load of people without geographic obstacles. It is wonderful, but hang in there please, the best and worst is yet to come...

Picture, please, the following tragic illusion. It is an illusion of 'sharing', using online blogging. There is some excellent writing online, some bloggers with a fair number of readers and some vibrant interaction. Some people host visual galleries alongside their writing. Some of them connect people with similar interests and expertise across the globe. But here's the illusion. It's an illusion that strikes ordinary folk who are trying but failing to connect with other ordinary folk in real life community. They may have a unique take on the world, or be experts in some narrow field. They might be sociable and extrovert. Whatever, they would like to get a bit of human connection, like so many of us. If they don't, they fear they'll end up talking to themselves in the street. They see no easy way to achieve connection in the world of real people in physical spaces. So they turn to the digital inferno. They set up camp on *Facebook*, on *Twitter* or start a blog on *Word Press* or *Blogger*. They join discussion groups and chat rooms. One or two of their friends and family may know they are struggling with loneliness. So they become flag-waving avid readers of their blog.

Or do they? I've heard friends of a certain chap say that they always 'like' his posted poems, but rarely read them right through.

Several make a comment intended to assure him that he is not speaking into the void. I've no doubt this happens in the physical realm, and many probably learned this behaviour there first. In the digital realm a facsimile of comradeship, with nothing behind it, is endemic.

If you have a wish to connect with a broader range of people, then take an honest look at your online social whirl. How many friends have you really got? Who is really responding to you, connecting with you? Of course the hugs are all there but if it is real hugs you ache for, making do with those virtual ones saps your will-power for getting them, in a slow trickle, dripping out so slowly it isn't noticed.

What if *no one* is actually reading your blog? What have you got? What do the 'likes' really mean? How meaningful are they? If it's all a bit of fun, sure ... but how much of that commitment pays off and helps to solve the real problem of isolation? If it is better than nothing and you have reasons for accepting this in your life, then no one is trying to spoil the party. If you have a wish (and a will behind that wish) to walk along deep in conversation with others by your side, to a café where you'll meet up with other friends, and where you'll sometimes meet interesting new people as well ... then if no one is actually reading your blog, let it all go. If you have that wish and a will which is loyal to your interests, then you just might give up checking in to an empty platform. Find the platform where the trains come in and take you to some real people.

I have seen whole departments and organizations in the business world succumb to the illusion that they are *not* talking to themselves. Post after post goes up on discussion boards and on microblogging platforms such as *Yammer* and the same few people respond. They collect duff statistics of 'thousands of hits' which, in reality, are search engines or people who spend no more than a few seconds on the page. They talk it up, convince themselves they are popular when, in reality, they are at a dance where the band didn't show. There are blogs where the blogger is also the main responder! I know one blogger who set up extra email addresses in order to use the alternative identities to make his blog posts look more popular.

Platforms such as *Yammer* and *Word Press* offer genuine opportunities for publishing, feedback, learning and shared decision-making but, as always, getting results requires skill, effort and groundwork. Of course, online activity links people with the social glue for maintaining some real community experience but it's just a lot rarer than the hype would suggest.

I'd like to suggest that microblogging in many cases just sidesteps the harder challenge of physically connecting with a few people in an authentic way. The worst thing to do, for those who have an ache for real contact, is to enter into the illusion sustained by counting how many responded with a 'like' to their latest single line post. So many posts go completely unanswered, while some blogs and discussion boards stoop to recycling the same few people day after day after day, which is just too, too similar to that lonely man talking to himself in the street.

We are born for authentic connection. We are born with eyes to look for the soul in the eyes of others. We are born with fingertips for touching and detecting fine distinctions of texture. For actual contact we need to reach out and touch others with eyes and hands. Sure, we can touch others online if the connection is authentic and warmed by genuine motives. But if we have cooked up a fantasy built from some off-the-cuff likes and fingertip friends on *Facebook*, then we are crying in the wilderness. This happens in the real social world too but less so, no doubt because reaching out in the real world requires greater effort, and failure is too self-evident. One-click virtual touching fills the social jar with a lot of nothing. Soon enough, *Facebook* timelines are going to look like tragic stories about loneliness which are as desperate as taking momentary eye contact for friendship or confusing bumping into someone on a train with a hug.

Try this: take an honest look at your timeline

Look at some 'timelines'. Too many are a monologue of recycled dreams with lots of swaying alone to a slow tune on the dance floor of life. How is the timeline of your life shaping up? How much is your digital timeline enriching you, developing you, and deepening your connections with other people? How much time are you putting in and is what you are getting out justifying the investment? Grab some paper and list your most recent activity – the tasks completed, the posts, the people connected to, the comments you contributed. How do all of these serve your personal growth and development, and the realization of your aims in life?

The virtual world is a counterpoint to the physical. Social media often borrows the terms of physical connection though, of course, the digital versions of 'hug', 'friend' and 'sharing' have a lower rate of value. Such connectedness is functional rather than spiritual. The real world has higher requirements when it comes to being actually connected to others. Friendship is earned and deeply given, something which is best learned when we are young.

So if you are kissing your *Facebook* connections 'goodnight' and comforted by the warmth of the battery, if this keeps loneliness at bay, then my words have nothing to say to you. If you seek communion with others through your eyes, your smile and the sweet silences that come with closeness and trust, then you might have to kick the online drug. It becomes less effective over time anyway.

Time for an honesty check: who is reading your blog? Really? And when you 'share', are you sharing with anyone? How much caring connection is there – from you and for you – in the online swirl? What is the quality of it? The thing may satisfy the craving for distraction but does it satisfy the need to be connected? What if your social media 'story' is a digital case of *walking along and talking to yourself* syndrome?

11

The Attack on Memory — Dancing Back into Sacred Remembering

The dramatic heading refers to what some might think is a harmless phenomenon. This is the deliberate restriction on social media platforms of a bit of functionality that used to be taken for granted and is still a basic feature on laptops and personal computers but is starting to disappear from the 'cloud' and social media platforms that we increasingly use to create and store our files. This is the function of deleting.

And I mean delete. Erasing something so it is gone, as if you had burned it or shredded it. We assume we can do this. It has shocked many people when I've informed them that what they think they are deleting is now 'archived'. It's being made harder and, in some cases virtually impossible, to delete a file. Instead, it is hidden away in a 'vault' whether you want that or not. Currently my email and social networking applications on my phone give me no option to delete. One allows me to 'archive', the other not even that.

Delete something so it is irretrievable? I'm very sorry sir, we can't allow that.

Well, imagine you put something in your rubbish bin and the bin spits it out. Imagine if you discovered that all of your rubbish was being stored somewhere. Imagine you write down some thoughts and decide that you want to throw it away. Imagine you put the paper in a shredder but it relays it onto the archive shelf instead. You might actively want the letter to cease to exist. This is not at all uncommon I would imagine. *Sorry, no. We'll keep it for you.*

The right to delete is being taken away from us, right under our noses, and often with our collusion even. You cannot delete a message on *Facebook* – you are given only the option to 'archive' it. Want to delete it forever? Want to insist? You can't. The provider of the service has decided to serve its own (not always stated) goals before your own. They are your files and thoughts but it has been decided that they will be kept, somewhere, whether you will it or not.

Purging things from our lives – such as actually burning them – is a form of cleansing. If our past is kept somewhere whether we like it or not then the inner relief of the cleansing fire is denied. The fire symbolically (and with certainty) puts the matter behind us in a way which clears and braces the mind.

Discarding what went before is vital to our creative flow and has always been seen as good for refreshing our onward journey. We can discard and reboot ourselves as a completely new being, unlike the computer. We move through time as a growing thing and can recreate ourselves by leaving something behind. We need to know, at many levels, that we can move on. It's a practice for our inner health. It can help us achieve peace of mind, resolution and future growth.

We also need to be able to forget in order to remember what we actually do need to remember. The actress needs to forget how she practised her lines in order to let them flow on the stage. The artist discards a previous work and starts a new canvas to take the kernel of past experience into something new. And when we delete our files their particular content vanishes but we take the essence forwards in a new way.

I would like to suggest that we need to be able to destroy certain things in order to grow and change. It is a human necessity. Putting things into an archive is altogether quite different to really letting them go for good. Imagine you have a clear-out, a big bonfire to follow in the garden. It is going to feel good, because the physical clearing out will help to clear you out inside too, psychologically and emotionally. Now imagine the flames just will not burn what you have put onto the fire. You watch the flames but when they have died down the old stuff is all still there.

Our memory is being interfered with by removing the right to delete. We are offered 'timelines' on social media platforms but denied control of the material — our material — which is on them. So it is no longer really ours. That is what one must conclude from the behaviour of the proprietors of these platforms, no two ways. But creativity grows through making mistakes and then leaving them behind. If we can't delete, i.e. let go, forget and move on with courage, then we will *create cautiously*. We will be in a self-contradicting predicament, that of trying to pre-empt our spontaneity. There are psychiatric reports of just this kind of condition.

I hope that one day we will look back on the days when corporations tried to lay claim to what we wanted to delete and forget as an evil time. As they cleverly refine the system we may find that deletion becomes a premium priced product. Of course, they presented the imposition of archiving with the loss of deleting as something benevolent. Are all of us missing something here? At the same time? Because benevolence does not behave that way. It has goodwill and goodwill usually respects rights. Of course, given the choice, we might just choose *delete* and that would spoil the game plan of the 'timeline' paranoids with their fear of gaps outside their control. The task of truly hiding your 'timeline' is set up so that attempting to will probably tire you out. Why I wonder? Was it technically that difficult to make it straightforward?

You have no problem with not being allowed to delete? It is obviously a personal choice. Those of you who *do* want the right to permanently discard the thoughts, images and feelings which you have committed to the digital realm will need to unsubscribe from certain platforms. This applies also to the online virtual tools which keep an indelible record of everything you've ever shared online. At the very least you will need to be a lot more selective about what you share 'out there' in the first place. You'll need to become more discerning and wary of signing up to services that won't let you burn your own stuff.

To 'archive' should be a free choice among others which include 'delete forever' and 'save'. In some way that matters but is hard to express, we have been manoeuvred into being unable to ever truly forget. Our online trace is kept. It is creepy. If you cannot discard what you need to, a binding chain grows around you which you can't take off. And each digital action is another link in the chain. What about rebirth, the lightness of being we discover from personal growth and the clean page which has no indents or smudges coming through from the one you just tore off the pad?

Thankfully, you can 'mega'-delete at present. But do you have the will to? If you want to let go and win back your free flow, mega-deleting the convenient online dwelling which you have grown so used to may be your only option.

12

Digital Gesturing and the Smiley

The practice of using the 'smiley' has enormously increased the sharing of information about our emotional state with others. We aren't physically present with others when we use them so they cannot see our real smile. So we show them what our face (or body) is doing with an icon. It is very simple to do and to understand. Well, you might think it was that simple. And it could be. Many people, before computers were invented, used emotional icons (emot-icons) in their letter writing. They might sign a letter with a happy face as well as a name. Or they might put a sad face.

The key thing here is that what you are showing in the form of an emoticon is a symbol of what you are really feeling – truly feeling. Why would you use an icon which misrepresents what you are feeling? Yet that is exactly what many people do when they choose a smiley or type *LOL*. They insert a smiley, but they aren't physically smiling. They type *LOL* but they aren't actually laughing out loud.

The only way to place digital gestures is truthfully. They become an authentic representation of a true state; a smiley for your real smile or *LOL* because you really are laughing out loud. The golden rule is to never use a digital gesture that doesn't accurately stand for what you might truthfully express in person. Yet people text *LOL* all the time when they aren't laughing out loud. Why is this?

Neil's diary . . .

She arrived in Mumbai and that's it for three weeks now. I don't want to do Skype every night and we've agreed not to. I know we are going to miss each other, and I'm glad she's doing the course. We talked of writing each other one real letter a week, on real paper. I sat down to write mine and had the rather appalling realization that the muscles in my fingers must have just about wasted away, because my writing hand was tired after just four lines! Then it was midnight, two days after she'd arrived. I was missing her, trying to finish the letter – three pages long. Then a text came through. It was the shortest text she had ever sent me. It had two words on it and no 'X'. These were the two words: 'Miss you'. I found myself saying them out loud and smiling. I was glad there was no 'X' – just those two words. Two essential words. It was a full minute before I typed 'Miss you' in reply, then pressed 'send'. That was it. And if you are far away, sometimes that is all you need. A week later, I sent the letter by post.

Sometimes the conversation is an imagined role play with the play happening inwardly. My avatar may laugh more, and more loudly than the real me. I may not be laughing out loud but I am laughing inside and so the *LOL* reflects *that* state. It's an interesting state of affairs though because often, when we are chatting digitally, we are trying to show what might be taking place on the outside, physically. We hope a smile online means a real smile but that hope is caught in a conflict when we make our avatars engage in well-intentioned fakery which project more expressive versions of ourselves which laugh more, smile more and cry and hug all the time. Where is our truth in this? It is in there somewhere, sometimes, but it is so easy for it to turn into something else right under our fingertips.

We should set a standard of authenticity for ourselves. We would if we were aching for authenticity in return, for then we would naturally want the digital gestures we receive to reflect what is true. Your next kiss has to be one which has a meaning which you genuinely intend and believe will be well received. If we kiss digitally when we don't truly intend it, or when we know it would never be accepted by the other in the real world, then we dilute the meaning of that gesture. It becomes a dead routine. None of these things is necessarily wrong in all cases, but if we ourselves are not truthful, then we collude in a lowering of standards and each digital gesture will be about as good as a little white lie. If the role play is intended and entered into by both parties, then fun can ensue. We can play at being different and even at being more than we really are in the physical world. However, when this is done in ways that delude others we can contribute to deception and a cheapening of relationships. Role play can soon become power play and avatars can become actors in a dark fantasy.

Some will surely say that blurring our message in any way we wish is liberating and helps us to flow more and reduces inhibitions. People can feel uplifted and even turned on by the typed kiss. In time a 3D-printed, lifelike copy of someone's lips will be animated and deliver a version of the real thing. This will come, sooner than we think. And now your own instincts must judge whether this matters at an essential level. If you feel that this technological path is not one you want to travel down, then consciously placing your digital gestures and using them authentically helps to set the standard. Your foundation in the digital inferno will be truthful when you ensure that your inner gestures and your outer behaviours are in harmony with each other. An X means a real kiss, or you don't X.

False air kisses from pretentious friends amount to the same thing. Isn't this the same as faking in the digital world? There certainly is an overlap here. There's plenty of fakery in both worlds and the message regarding both has to be the same: to return to what feels authentic and to make kisses and smiles sincere. This would keep role-playing within bounds so that no one is being deliberately fooled, including yourself.

Yet, when we are interacting digitally, and unscrutinized by others, there is more scope to be inauthentic. If we scowl while typing a smiley there is no one there to see. The digital realm lends itself more easily to deception and self-deception – deception of others because we can hide behind the screen and deception of ourselves when we value false feedback. I look into a mirror which tells me that I am the fairest of them all and congratulate myself on 20 digital kisses.

The digital realm removes the danger of being rumbled when our faces betray what we really feel. We can also avoid the dangers of being misconstrued with no-nonsense and often humorous smileys. There are dark versions too; we can throw-up, shoot ourselves in the head or explode. There is frequent exaggeration intended to convey a grain of truth; so an animated flood of tears stands for disappointment. We know this is seen for what it is, so we send an exaggerated emoticon which, we hope, will at least register as a single tear.

We might, of course, reach out to those we yearn to receive understanding from in sincere, carefully worded thoughts. Is digital interaction being reduced to something bland by all this? Does it reduce the emotional palette to a child's tray of paints and a few primary colours? The prize for this is remote digital connection. The prize is that you can role play an idealized self from your sofa.

When our gesture is authentic the emoticon assumes true value. The authenticity gives value to sender and receiver. Our digital experiences seem deeper and richer. We may also find that we meet more. A genuine wish to see someone, expressed in authentic text kisses, matures into the will to get out and do it. Soon, weekly typed contacts with Grandma become an actual visit. It might even be an uncomfortable and awkward journey but, at the end of it, there she is! And we might say to ourselves, 'This is what life tastes like, both bitter and sweet together.'

Let's get practical.

Try this: go for authentic simplicity

Try this for a day, or a week, and see how it goes. Resolve to only ever make digital gestures that you would truly express physically. Don't put a smiley if you aren't smiling. Don't put an X unless there really would be kissing (of some kind) with the person. Choose mindfully and truthfully. Observe the reactions in you and in others. If someone offers you an X, don't offer one back unless you mean it and think you really would be permitted to give it in person.

You might feel that this is all spoiling the fun. Too earnest, not 'cool'. Too sober. Be patient and persevere. Soon you may find an electric moment which is suddenly real and vital – not a 'wow' moment but a subtle one, for reflecting on. There is no mystery here. Authenticity is a real force emanating from people. It is a truth in us which makes the words true. What flows between us guides relationships in subtle ways, and if what flows is authentic it flows all the more. When you really place your gestures with all this in mind you will be more in control, more present and interactions will have another dimension.

Try this: watch out for habits

Over the next day or two, notice how you end messages. Did you go 'cool' or LOL or XXX? Look for habitual use of certain phrases or emoticons. Let some spontaneity loose on your little band of habits. But spontaneous does not mean 'without thinking'. Try replacing habits with what you actually think, first of all by reflecting on what that might actually be. You will come up with things that are fresh and new, in *that* moment, relating to *that* person. It will take longer and will interrupt your flow of habits. Be patient and go with it. Soon you will find that a more multi-faceted self is showing itself – fresher, more alive and more you. Banish the automatic response. Recall that behind the words you receive is another person who is the centre of his or her own universe just like you are of yours. Value that person with an authentic response.

Perhaps it is time to go 'cold turkey' with the emoticons.

Try this: a day with no emoticons at all, no digital gestures

Simply 'speak' and write with the effort to be mindful. Call the person to mind in your memory. Picture them, not just physically either. This is about getting back to essential thoughts and feelings, not dressed up with easily thrown out emoticons and simplified gestures. Put what you feel inside into words. *Feeling inside* comes first. Then you let the words speak. This slows you down and you might even get writer's block. After a while, your words will feel brighter and more yours because they will emerge from your own inner life. You'll be empowered by the power of expression. Words will seem more valuable and effective when a smiley becomes a *thank you*, a frowning emoticon is replaced by a clear statement of why you are disappointed and a winking one becomes a clever little teaser of a line. Emoticons can be like ready meals but we can start to enjoy the taste of real home cooked food.

When we are speaking to someone but looking elsewhere, as if distracted, the listener does not feel properly acknowledged and can feel neglected or insulted even. Now this may seem strange, but when we send a text message in the same absent or distracted way the data might travel along fibre optic cables and through the air but our actual gesture does not. Authenticity reveals itself!

Over the years I have noticed that the use of authentic gestures, on stage in the theatre, when done well by performers, really adds to the power of the drama. The effect is more compelling when there is control and boldness in how the actors move and speak. When it is all rather undefined because the actor does not create it with intention first, then the gesture doesn't go anywhere, not even as far as the audience a few yards away. So, if I am in London and you are in Edinburgh, there are a few hundred physical miles between us.

As I press 'send', I imagine you across the space, geographically distant but still in the same realm as me, and I direct my intention and my gesture, my message and its meaning, across space and not through the screen. I might even turn my gaze away from the screen and look towards where I imagine you to be. We put a gesture into the real world though we send it via the digital realm. What we are doing by making a willed gesture is attaching importance to the relationship we have with that person. The technology will deliver the message while we are being mindful of the relationship across that distance. (I'm not suggesting anything psychic or paranormal is going on here, though it might be.) Otherwise it is all abstract, and abstraction is a place which the digital realm is really good at keeping us in.

The ease with which we can text each other can dim our awareness of the importance of seeing each other physically. Feeling the physical distance and the separation can ignite the will which moves physical feet to undertake a real visit.

Try this: dive into the digital inferno and immerse yourself

Try a day of using as many emoticons, digital gestures and icons as possible. Use as much text shorthand as you can (*LOL* etc.) and immerse yourself in the medium. Give yourself permission to role play and be whatever avatar you want. At the end of the day look back and read your various digital interactions. How did it feel and how does it feel now? How present were you, how conscious? What was gained and what was lost? How authentic did it all seem?

The digital realm is a new space and there's a new artistry in the freedom of digital gesturing, role playing and projecting one's avatar. Some love it and hold their own pretty well. Some people use digital gadgetry but hold back from diving in fully. A day spent diving in can be a revealing experience. If you are seeking to hold your own as *you* in the digital realm then immersion in a state of self-abandonment can reveal some shocking perspectives. Diving in, in that way, may actually fire up your will to climb out for good.

Digital gesturing is a new form of theatre, and theatre is acting. Confident actors can step into role and then step out of the costume at the end of the day. For many others, we can lose our essential self-awareness and control by acting without quite knowing what we are doing. Emoticons offer us punch lines which are ready for grabbing on to and, because we are all using them, the threshold for audience approval is fairly low. Kisses fly all over the place and we exchange tenderness and subtlety for giggles. As we get better at it we can become skilled at our chosen role, and a well-timed smiley can deliver a sinister undertone of threat or smugness, whilst a carefully measured number of kisses, such as *XX*, communicates pique because the third one is left out. But our coded messages can sow confusion. The drama becomes an epic with ongoing dialogue amounting to an emotional roller-coasting soap opera. We can literally forget who we are while the epic takes over. The actor forgets to take off the costume.

And seasoned experts in the digital realm have learned how to use smileys and digital gestures in order to manipulate. There is ruthlessness behind the emoticons of the online businessman who can use them to perfection for prompting compliant responses from customers. Such a fellow uses the thumbs-up for approval when the objectives are being met and an emoticon of tears when they are not. The aim, of gaining our compliance, is hidden.

A smiley is simple and it isn't an accident that its colours are usually bright. Our personal, unique head shape is standardized into a circle and the smile is a no-nonsense, one-dimensional diagram. This simplification wipes out ambiguity which can lend a feeling of power to the smiler. We can smile unequivocally with our smiley while our real inner state is actually confused, or far more complex. We might use a smiley like laying down an ace, in the hope of giving the impression that we are holding a winning hand.

Smileys say, 'Take this! For this is me!' This simplification asserts a standard value whether it is a real one or a bluff. Then conversation becomes a blend of truth, insincerity and wishful thinking.

So, here's the paradox. On the one hand, the use of a smiley can simplify and clarify. It can make the role play flow. The false smiles may even inspire real ones, drawing us onwards and upwards. On the other hand, we can simplify in the way that caricatures simplify. When we pretend we are what we are not, in the hope that the pretence will give birth to what we'd rather be, we lose. Emoticons speed up a certain kind of communication by cutting it down to simplified, pre-set forms. At the same time, they give us false images of each other because something true and precious, which is perhaps more complex and difficult to reach, can be missed. We probably can all identify with the problems. We can all help to set a better standard.

Maybe you dived in so deep and so long ago that you are wondering what all the fuss is about? Sure, there is no fuss, unless you've personally had enough. If you feel that spending hours a day on digital posturing is too much drama and not enough of the real thing, well and good. It might just be time to pull off the costume, get off stage and out onto the street for a bit of the live version of life.

13

Staying Safe and Secure in the Digital Inferno

We could be hacked into at any time. Our bank details are not safe. Money can leak out of our account at the whim of some teenage genius on the other side of the planet. Sexual predators are poised in cyber disguise ready to pounce on our kids. Bogus websites sell us fake goods, dangerous medicines and take cash from us without delivering. These are not myths. They are regularly reported and the statistics are mostly heading skywards. Buying is one click or free phone call away. Complaining is by snail mail or a call to a premium phone number. When we buy a product or service we are treated as a virtual VIP. When there's a technical problem, we are directed to online forums. We try to filter search results so our kids don't see porn or disturbing images but some of it always gets through.

This is just some of the dark side of the digital inferno – the flip side of instant access to information, crowd funding, inspiring gaming, finding lost friends, online petitions that change decision makers' minds, and of all that fun, creative expression and publishing potential in the hands of anyone with a gadget. It is light and shadow, good and evil and the space in between. The whistle-blowers and rebel hackers may just turn out to be the saviours by waking us up to a dark side that threatens to wipe out privacy and gives corrupt leaders the means for realizing quite sinister goals. The criminals, saints, freedom fighters, vigilantes, predators, they are all in there.

Far too many of us still have too little understanding of this all-encompassing swirl. Too many people have insufficient protection on their home and work-based devices, probably because of a lack of understanding of how they really work. They get the reality check when the fraudsters call and cream off their bank accounts or destroy files on the hard drive. Most households have some kind of virus on one of their devices. Some have been hijacked by 'botnets' (automated digital robots that can redirect some of the processing power of a computer to unsavoury ends). Many viruses, worms and spyware (don't you just love the rich and varied terminology?) are fairly harmless. But the new threat is cyber-terrorism and cyber war in which the vital operating systems of industry, the military, communications networks and banks are remotely manipulated. This means nuclear reactors, missiles and the whole nightmare. The dangers are often played down by the corporations at the heart of the digital realm. Then they discover that their own systems are compromised and they have to issue apologies to their customers that personal data has been stolen.

The seeds grew into plants years ago. The digital inferno is a garden of beautiful scented blooms, Venus' flytraps and poisonous weeds. More spring up all the time and if you don't know your way through the jungle, then you are a ready target for the predator. The actual target might be someone close to you, with you caught in the crossfire.

It could be that your inbox just fills up with newsletters you don't want to read, or that corporations analyse your online behaviour and target you with offers of products and services, and even trick you into signing up for something you don't need. Or that your personal information is stolen and used, your identity taken and sold on or used for fraud. Or that your children gain access to images and content that could make them insensitive or psycho-logically scar them for life.

In some ways the current digital maelstrom reminds me of a lawless frontier town of a few hundred years ago. The digital realm outpaces any efforts to have oversight of it. It is constantly expanding and the law makers are often running three steps behind the criminals. Some of its biggest players feel there should be few or no laws at all. The corporations are at the heart of it all and behind nearly all of what goes on in there. Much of our creative freedom is still nestled in that corporate cage. The outer edges of the inferno (the parts we are in when we are looking for what's on at the cinema or buying a plane ticket) follow a simple method for increasing revenue. It needs high click rates and people of all ages, from as young as possible, online and maximizing revenue.

This isn't a conspiracy theory, only a brief description of a new continent that defies exploration and mapping because it changes while it is mapped. So, where does that leave you, the parent, the individual and the local group? Knowing how the digital realm works, at least at a basic level, must be good for us. A bit of time spent getting wise to the mechanics raises our ability to play in it more safely, and to say *yes* and *no* when we want to. Without doubt, we need to be as secure as we can, because the threat of fraud and identity theft is real. There are packages around – some free, some premium, that can offer us a certain level of safety from attack.

But you know all this. What I am adding to the picture is a plea that we be more mindful. It isn't enough to buy the burglar alarm and switch it on, because the digital realm is already watching our behaviour as we click away at our keyboards thinking that we are in the privacy of our own home. We can keep out the illegal burglars but how do we keep out the legal time stealers who tempt our kids with sexualized adverts, and the products and services with small print too small to read and too bamboozling to understand? Too many people click *accept* to the terms and conditions which they neither read nor would understand if they did. If they aren't important, why are we forced to accept them? If they are important, why are they 60 pages long and written in legal and technical gobbledegook?

Do we give up and surrender? Do we flee? I can't give you a solution but I can share my experience. Just like a real country, the digital realm now has its own resistance movements. With effort, you can block ads, limit what your kids see, turn off alerts and notifications, check out the credentials of web-based sellers and even find demystified versions of terms, conditions and warnings. You will need to hunt around and be a bit of a detective, but wouldn't you do that if you were visiting a dangerous city?

To be safe in there you need to be able to hold your own. And your best tool for that is to be conscious, alert and under no illusions: the dangerous neighbourhoods in the digital realm can be as brightly lit as theme parks and shopping malls.

In the digital world, thinking is a kind of walking. Thinking moves us across the new frontier and into digital territory. Giving inadequate forethought to what seems a simple journey makes it more likely that we will stray into danger. There are ways to keep you and your kids safer in this miraculous and perilous space. Some of these ways are about learning to stay detached and getting some objectivity. Often you'll need to approach a decision from different viewpoints. Thus, you don't buy something until you've read reviews. This means reviews of the product, and of the seller, and maybe even of the website doing the reviews. You might need to check that a download doesn't contain a virus or that a website is safe for your kids to view. In the digital realm you will need to be prepared to look for confirming or conflicting evidence in order to tell truth from the lies. Here's a quotation from Howard Rheinghold who writes on the internet.

Digital media and networks can empower only the people who learn how to use them – and pose dangers to those who don't know what they are doing. Yes, it's easy to drift into distraction, fall for misinformation, allow attention to fragment rather than focus, but those mental temptations pose dangers only for the untrained mind. Learning the mental discipline to use thinking tools without losing focus is one of the prices I am glad to pay to gain what the Web has to offer.

Try this: a Digital Safety Check before making a purchase

You want to buy a new tennis racket. Search for 'tennis racket' via a search engine and then choose a website which offers them. Then work through the following little 'safety model':

1. Check its credentials

Do a second search under the website name and any owning company you can find. Look for reports of being scammed or defrauded by this site. Look for reports on customer service (look for more than one). Seek out *independent* sites that review this seller. Look for a logo and evidence that it is a trusted seller (although these can all be faked, they are better than nothing).

2. Check its appropriateness

Click through a few links and ensure that any targeted adverts or hosted images are of the kind you'd want your children to see. If the images are too adult then buy the product when children are not present.

3. Do a price and quality comparison

Where possible, check to see if the price, especially if low, seems realistic. Look for hidden costs. Ensure that the product isn't being shipped from a country known for product faking and copying. Check for originality of source.

4. Check with your instincts

These are your best guide and we tend to forget them when staring at a bright computer screen.

This is just an example. The key thing here is clear thinking. Keeping yourself and your loved ones safe in the digital realm may well involve slowing down, stepping back to reflect more often and being cautious and curious. It doesn't mean negativity and mistrust as the default but it does mean not confusing being conscious with boring, fruitless effort. Life demands, in every realm and not just online, that we sharpen our wits now. Some of the thrill of the free-ranging immersion you get from being online presents the same risk level that goes with deep-water diving, or surfing without local knowledge of the currents and rocks. You don't leave your front door wide open whilst heading off somewhere else, because of the risk of burglary. That is an easy risk to foresee. I am trying to show that heading off somewhere else online has similar risks.

Safety includes safe working online. Make sure the spaces where you work allow you to sit with your back and your neck aligned and upright, not prone to strain and injury further along your physical timeline. A good friend of mine who runs a web design company went through years of surgery and pain to try to sort out his wrist injury as a direct result of too much work at a desk that let his wrist hang in mid-air as he typed and clicked for hours for £11 an hour. He sued his employer and never got a penny. Get smart. Get informed and ensure your physical arrangements around your digital devices will keep you and your loved ones safe and, if you are an employer, free from court action.

Again, this is all nothing new. Office work existed before computers. Factory work, mining and agriculture destroyed a lot of backs, wrists and lungs. Eyes working in poor candlelight were strained till they were blind. But computer work brings new problems, and to people as young as toddlers. Risks have intensified and new ones have emerged. Welcome to squinting, arthritis of the thumb and backache. Welcome to migraines, after-image dreaming, nightmares and repetitive strain. Many of us walk through this realm unaware of the risks. They are under-researched (and therefore under-reported), underplayed and even denied. So, how were you sitting last time your attention was fixed on a task on the screen? Are you heading for stooped old age? Did you just sit up straight? How's your back or your neck?

Let's end this chapter with a boring activity that might just save your digital and physical lives.

> **Try this: the boring but life-saving checklist**
>
> Work through this check list and tick off as many as possible or write 'done' next to them.
>
> 1. Virus-check all of your digital devices and update your virus checker.
> 2. Ensure all of your passwords are secure and not guessable and *don't use the same one for everything.*
> 3. Use data encryption whenever you can.
> 4. Don't store your bank details online or on your devices.
> 5. Make sure your firewall is switched on, on all devices.
> 6. Put appropriate filtering on your devices to protect your children from harm.
> 7. Ensure your children are clued up and can talk to you about their digital realm worries and fears and any trouble they might be having. Clue them in to staying safe.
> 8. Cancel your subscription to any services you don't trust and that might be passing on your data to third parties.
> 9. Ensure you've said *no* to having your details passed on to third parties by any services you have remained joined to and learn about the various privacy settings for services you access.
> 10. Don't let any services publish details of when you are absent from home, and don't publish personal phone numbers and addresses online unless you know exactly what you are doing.

It can be a chore to have to lock the doors and windows before we go out for the day. There are still places in the world where you don't have to do that but for most of us the lock-up ritual is simply part of the day.

Many hackers are after your digital identity and bank details, using them or selling them on. In all cases, the less mindful you are the more likely you are to be jumped on, just as in the real mean streets. And you'll only realize its awfulness when it happens to you. Keeping you and your family safe in the digital realm is clearly the smart thing to do, though a hacker can still find a way in if he really wants to. Hackers have found their way into highly encrypted parts of government and business systems, but most of us are relying on free or cheap online security that fails as much as it succeeds. Being hacked can feel as personally violating as being burgled. Many who have suffered that trauma were in the 'It will never happen to me' camp. Of course, hacking has different motives. Some antisocial member of Geeksville may be simply testing his genius against the latest security walls and you simply get caught up in the fun. Others are on a mission against the corporations, against governments, individuals and groups they disagree with. When some hacker strikes a blow for his idea of justice you might find yourself being among the collateral damage.

Keeping your children safe as they grow up is no longer just about the real streets. The digital realm is full of sexual predators. All of the beautiful streets in the digital realm are potentially mean streets. As it is mostly invisible to the unwary eye, danger is no longer confined to the dark alleys but lurks right out in the open. Keeping safe means caring about how our digital world impinges upon our real one.

We can feel laden with it all – overburdened with passwords, login details and conflicting versions of files copied in several places. We receive offers and newsletters from companies we bought something from years back or whose digital shop windows we browsed just once. We find we are still registered with services we can't seem to deregister from and, if we do manage to, we get emails begging us to come back. And, amongst all of that are offers, reminders, invitations and alerts which are one click away from installing a virus on our computers that can take it over without our knowing about it. On the even darker side, images of our kids on holiday, innocently posted on a social media site, are doing the rounds of paedophile rings and being sold. The load can feel too heavy. It is quite possible to wander into the digital realm without any protection at all. It's a lighter way to travel and involves carrying very little. It is often done under cover of anonymity. To do this, you must have nothing worth stealing and nothing worth damaging. Many digital burglars and criminals work in just that way.

Try this: lightening your digital load

Make a list of the things you value most in the digital realm. It might include your online banking, your store of films and photos, your blog. How protected and safe are they? Do you have them copied and backed-up somewhere else? Is there anything in your digital estate that would be better stored or located elsewhere, perhaps physically?

Doing a regular security check and having a think about what you have in there, how important it is to you and how secure it is, is a way to value yourself.

Try this: digital de-cluttering

The more doorways you create into your house, the more points of entry you create for the intruder. The more you have in there, the more there is to steal. Many people use easily guessable passwords – the same or similar ones, or ones that are too short. This is like having front door keys that are easy to copy and which fit other doors as well. Many join different platforms and sites and then forget to visit them while leaving their personal details still sitting there. Each site listing your details is another security breach opportunity. Each is another window waiting to be smashed. Carry out an inventory of all the things you have signed up to and have a good de-clutter. It improves your security and gives you peace of mind.

We routinely expose ourselves to the risks that accompany our enjoyment of things. But you can deal with those risks more consciously, whether snowboarding or surfing the web. When you do that, you are not only safer but more self-aware as a person.

14

Reclaiming the Whole Narrative

'The single most valuable resource I have is uninterrupted thought.'
Adam Brault

Yet again, I am going to run the risk of being a fuddy-duddy and a spoiler. I'm sure my critics will have long since come to the conclusion that that is just what I am. Permit me, please, to protest that I am a defender of the digital realm who merely wants to advocate a more conscious approach to it.

Thought for the day: stop commentating on the sidelines of your own peak experiences.

What on earth do I mean by that? Let me give an example or two. Someone is present at some significant event. It could be a concert, an Olympic final or their daughter's wedding. Say it's a candlelit dinner. Two people are taking tentative romantic steps towards each other. They are mutually engrossed and their attention is an unbroken flow, smooth like cream. But no! Out pops the mobile phone with some new stuff on *Twitter* or *Facebook*, or *LinkedIn. So what? It's all just a bit of innocent fun, isn't it?* Permit me to ask whether we have stopped noticing that interruption kills the flow. I sometimes wonder if we remember what flow is. The power of the whole is its 'whole'-istic nature. Interruption, for whatever reason, can knock the stuffing out of experiences which take time to unfold their full reality. Sure, we live on many levels at once but that fact also stands for a new kind of fragmentation. Seeing something through from start to finish is like healthy nature in us, like taking a deep breath in and then out. It is good for us, because it is deep in our nature. We can tear ourselves away from the flow of healthy rhythms if we so choose but the need for them will remain a part of us. Interrupting the breath all the time would disturb the nervous system and the rhythm of the heart. Wonderful rhythms tick away within us and hold us together. Countless rhythms of light, warmth and gravitation surround us and hold everything together. The plants and animals all obey them in their faithful, unconscious way. If you interrupt their processes by, for example, constantly digging up a plant to see how its roots are doing then it will not grow, though it will keep trying to the very last because it has an unbreakable flow of necessity working in it. Trust the roots. Interrupt the living flow and things will not grow.

When I go to a play, I might try to appreciate what's on offer in fits and starts and jumping all over the place inside. Unlike an animal, which has its own inner flow to obey, I must control my own inner flow of attention. If I do, then the play *grows* for me. If I immerse myself in the play by following it with an unbroken flow, I discover that giving myself in that way makes it a long, gorgeous breath of an experience that runs through my whole being. But many people these days find it impossible to stay focused on one thing for very long. Ironically, many computer games are designed to capture our attention with hypnotic force, and they do. A person can stare at a screen for an entire train journey yet be incapable of staying for the same length of time with a book or a conversation.

Reclaiming the whole narrative involves several competencies we may well have started to lose. One is the ability to stay with something out of our own will force. This means that we join the moments into a unity by inner activity. Another is being patient with a process. We grow slowly. Things of value grow slowly. Patience brings perseverance and both are necessary for realizing our goals in life.

It can be fun keeping our presence on our various networks current but the habit of commenting on the sidelines of our experience by constantly tweeting, texting and micro-reporting in real-time quietly develops a certain habit in us. It is the habit of rapidly shifting attention in response to what is coming at us, so that our attention is taken rather than consciously given. We stop giving the kind of attention which involves patient waiting, like the cat at the mouse hole. Rapid shifts of attention deprive us of sensing the wholeness of something and feed back on us to make us feel fragmented. This fragmentation is like our will-power going on and off. It seems fair to suppose that, as a result of this habit becoming widespread amongst us, we will feed it with the increasing compulsion to 'package' experience as a series of interrupted or rapidly changing smaller units. We can 'chunk' the song into sound bites but the real song will not be there any more and we can chunk life into sound bites but real life will not be there anymore.

All right, please, don't think I don't get that live commentary on a micro-blogging platform is great fun. But I've met too many people who missed a glorious solar eclipse because they were engrossed in trying to photograph it. I've been at an incredible musical performance where someone was texting away so much he rarely looked up and couldn't possibly have followed the flow of the music. Giving ourselves up to the full, uninterrupted experience lends it a sacred quality. Instead of having to be hit over the head by something before we get it we can begin to respond to what is rare, fine and precious. And we grow smarter, I think, because feedback from joined up attention helps to join us up inside.

Interrupting a process, especially one that is important, is always a possibility, but it should be a conscious choice. We should interrupt it because we will it, not because we are 'pulled' away and it does not occur to us to resist. I might read a book from cover to cover without a pause because that's what I need at that moment. It's the book that goes deep, like one gorgeous breath of experience, and even changes my life. I start walking and keep going, and it's energizing, and something shifts in my thinking which brings towards me a new experience of myself to grow into. We begin, keep going, and a flow emerges which wants to play out to its natural end – *start* and *finish* sometimes do not want an interrupted middle.

Interruption should always be a productive choice. Sometimes we put our paintbrush down and interrupt our flow to rest or to seek a new focus for a time. When that is a real choice it refreshes us and feeds the quality of our flow. Writers take breaks all the time but then inspiration descends and they don't take breaks and the work flows on and on where it needs to, without interruption.

Being *always on* on our online devices, with an imagined audience of 'friends' and contacts supposedly depending upon minute by minute updates on our most important experiences, replaces one flow with another, inferior kind. The new flow is a commentary on our experiences: 'We interrupt this story with a newsflash.' Perhaps it is: 'I interrupt this life with a tweet.' Then we become real-time news reporters of experiences which deserve our full attention while they are actually happening. Sitting on the sidelines of our own experience splits the self between an *in-the-moment* one and one which *tries to capture it while it is happening.* We become tittle-tattle ghosts, haunted in the present moment by another self who lives in a mirror of social media, informers on our own secret selves.

Yes, I know it is innocent fun. But it isn't when it replaces our sense of being really present in our own lives.

Try this: calming constant commentary

Switch the device off, and give yourself a break. Experience without commenting. Let your networks know afterwards. You'll then find yourself in a different mode – not commentating on your thoughts but living into them and reflecting. In other words, getting to know yourself. When you do that you go into your experience and reap its harvest because you had a first-hand taste of its real content. Then switch back on at a moment which really fits into what you are up to. Feel your way towards just the one or two moments when you are at an event, or out and about, when something happens which has that spark which wants to arc to another person. Don't set your default to being 'ready to snap at any moment'. Place the device within your flow as a tool or a means to your own ends.

You are on a date. It's going well. Very well. Lots of smiling and some kissing. The next thing is supposed to be a mysterious silence, in which lots of things can well up, one of them being possibly a sense of oneness and trust. Instead, you *find yourself* heading to the bathroom – as if drawn by invisible threads – and your fingers are tapping 'Woohoo!', and you just have to change your status to 'In a Relationship' or 'It's complicated'. Was that what the smiling and kissing and the trust was for, to give you something to put on your page? Well, no. You return to your friend, wanting to pick up where you left off, to pick up the flow of what was unfolding. But the tweet has turned you into a twit, and the flow is broken. And unless you can weed your digital garden, that tweet will be there for eternity and may even show up on search engines.

Silence and flow are golden. If you are fractured, distracted or just elsewhere then the people you are with will feel it. It would be odd if they didn't.

Let your next peak experience be a whole one. Taste it all, without interruption. Don't become a live news bulletin for your dreams as they are coming true. And then later, at a time which feels right, when you have breathed in and breathed out, tasted and savoured, fashioned eloquent word pictures, you might share some things with others, as publicly or privately as you choose. When you get clued up on the digital realm's defaults as well as its possibilities it can become a brilliant vessel for sharing your thoughts, images, news and questions. Once again, all of this is not at all about the big bad internet. It is not about *not* using it but about *placing* it.

15

Parenting in the Digital Inferno

This is a topic for a whole book, so I offer my apologies for just writing a short chapter on such an important subject.

Some parents seem to believe it is their duty to drag their children as early as possible into adult life. They dress them up in adult costume. They hold adult conversations with them and treat them as if they are fully formed grown-ups in little bodies. This, with young children of two or three years.

'Would you like to come with mummy to the shops, or shall we leave it until tomorrow and stay in today?'

So what? I'll answer that with a question. How about the idea that addressing children as adults awakens adult tendencies in children before they are ready to come out naturally? Forcing them ahead before they are ready is like pulling off the outer layer of a bud before it is ready. Most of all, children need to unfold at their own speed and crucial to that is having the freedom to learn by exploring and playing. That is an old bit of parenting wisdom that many now seem to ignore. Time to play and dream allows the young child to develop in its proper time. Peeling off the sepals before the bud opens of its own accord reveals all the tightly bound petals inside but then they just go brown and die.

Our current generation of kindergarten-age children may live until they are well over 100. What is the reason for hurrying them into adulthood? What is wrong with giving them the years of exploration and play which they need? The cost of not doing so is high.

The play of infinite possibility for a child is all around it. There are objects of every kind and lots to soak up by watching the doings of all the big people. The child does finger paintings, explores the garden, makes sounds on musical instruments … and her senses and faculties grow out towards the living world. The child's dreaming imagination goes right into the world and draws out its essential nature. This is because very small children do not feel set apart from people and things. As strongly self-conscious adults, we have mostly forgotten how we once lived in an enchanted world which we felt one with in a deep, unspoken way. Children express this in many childlike ways, in particular through pictures and imaginative games. These can have deep meaning and are not at all silly children's games. Allowing children to wake up gradually from this imaginative dreaming state makes them stronger in the long run. Far from being a duty, it is actually not our right to try to snap them out of that stage before their little nervous systems are ready.

Putting a tablet computer into the hands of a toddler directs it to a kind of play which is bounded, finished and limiting. Even drawing programs are limited to the number of pixels (even millions are finite). Children are deprived of the mysterious spaces in between and have no way of understanding what they are really doing. How, for the child, does the colour appear on the screen? The colour on the screen lacks immediacy compared to drawing a crayon over a big white page with the hand. When the child climbs onto a fallen branch the crack of a twig prompts her to orientate herself in three dimensions as she turns her head towards the sound. The sounds and smells of the forest surround her and fill her hungry senses. The screen, however, is a small oblong which presents the child with no smells, tastes, variations in touch or gross motor activity for learning coordination. Some digital systems, such as the *Wii*, encourage bodily movements which follow digitally replicated simulated ski runs, discos and jogging routes. These locate the child in a simplified rendition of the world and its subtle changes – wind and rain, rough and smooth, living and non-living, and other people reacting to the same nuanced complexity – are all absent. The digital experience for the child mostly concentrates upon the sense of vision but for all of its apparent variety it remains a very limited world. It all goes into the head and nervous system while the active imagination and the full range of the senses are more or less out of the picture. If we want children to really understand leverage and balance in their upper school physics lessons (and not just memorize formulas), then let them climb trees and play with planks while they are young. No plastic early learning gadgets are required.

The tablet PC presents the child with fairy tales, a kind of painting, information, music and lots and lots of images but it is still just a hard block. The child's other senses are hardly engaged. The breeze doesn't play across it as it does across real paper in such a telling way, ruffling it to reveal how light and responsive it is. The tablet focuses attention into a narrow beam. The eyes are fixed on one focal plane and bodily movements are simplified to the press of a fingertip. Everything from the tablet goes into the head. This is not how a child should be learning in the early years.

Digital games and images, it will be said, stimulate the imagination but they do this with finished pictures only. The pictures may certainly be impressive in themselves and yet still not be suitable fare for the small child. When the child meets too many images which are finished off its own powers of imagination do not develop because they are not called upon. Powerful, completed images cover up or drown out what is stirring within so that the child tends to become a passive onlooker. Powers of imagination, as meant here, are not about making up unreal or *childish* things. They are real forces of the soul which take hold of experience in the first place and then give it different layers of meaning. If a child grows up having experienced even a small degree of immersion in finished images – in TV, film and games – it will lose its natural ability to make its own inner pictures. A film presents the child with one visual version of a story in strong images. If a child sees a film before reading a book, the images appear before its inner gaze as it reads (or as the story is told to it) and stop it from forming its own pictures. The film images *get there first*. On the other hand, soft images in a book which flow into each other in a natural way do not push the emerging imagination back into the child. The child then retains the ability to actively form inner pictures which deepens the understanding of things much later. The small child who meets detailed, intense and completed images quickly becomes dependent upon them. If the child is pushed in the direction of ready-made images and mimicking intellectual tasks too early it hits adolescence ready-made for commercial culture. Since so much of the inferno is under the control of corporations it is no surprise that its potential for *grooming* children to become shoppers is well and truly exploited. The sense for the new is tuned to the novelties of marketed fashion. The child's own originality is hidden, even buried, and may never come out. When real originality dares to come forth it is seen as weird or eccentric.

Gadgets forcefully focus our gaze on a single plane; interacting with them demands us to make strategic choices nearly all of the time. They sharpen the thinking for making decisions within tightly defined parameters (and executing them with a pointed finger). If they are in the hands of a child in whom this kind of thinking is yet to emerge in the natural developmental sequence then the child loses out without ever knowing it. A lump of clay, some paint on a piece of wet watercolour paper, forays into nature, learning to bake, and being lifted up in themselves by stories of human goodness – these are far more friendly to a child's development than having to decide between binary options which unfold in a purely linear manner: this or that, on or off, win or lose.

If the child uses the computer for long periods he becomes impatient with play that demands more of him than the computer's familiar and limited scope. He acquires conceptions of things which are too rigidly formed. Goals become focused on a device which can be activated, ideally immediately, and deliver a ready-made experience. This is Generation Z – the generation with the digital in their DNA. Yes, I am presenting a negative aspect of the digital world. Children aren't ready for digital interaction until they are over ten, even if they appear to grasp it at three and become perfectly adept as they grow up. As I have attempted to show through the observations above, subtle things are lost when the child is not allowed to go through its natural stages of development. And other seeds are sown which appear in adulthood as the weeds of cliché. Instead of being an individual, the person becomes a variant on existing templates.

Our children grow up as very savvy, knowing more about our smartphone than we do. Digital gadgets call upon their ability to work things out quickly and fit the pieces of the puzzle together, and they give big rewards for doing so. But instead of reaching inside of themselves for the strengths to meet the challenges which flow towards them in play and real social life, children leap into this easier world of on-off, activated or deactivated, this menu or that menu, and start to know life only as a kind of gadget to be worked out and operated until a better gadget comes along. The child becomes clever and precociously alert with a quality of awareness attuned to the limits of the digital realm. It is heaved up, early, onto a ladder of progression that mimics working life and the world of earning.

All this began with TV programmes such as *Sesame Street*, which employed the skills of advertising for the benevolent motive of teaching kids to read by selling letters to them. We even had the soap opera of *Ernie and Bert*. Comics targeted children with products as far back as the 1940s and print-based comics are now loaded with adverts. Most of these are linked to competitions which involve texting or going online. Nearly all of the prizes are apps, games, robots and toys with a range of accessories which the child will then browse for online. The big prize is nearly always a kid-friendly tablet computer.

Children are addressed head on as consumers. *Groomed* to consume. Even where no money is involved, games often involve winning virtual coins, bonuses and other ways to spend. It's an easy step for children to start thinking that what they want is what they need. Then the pressure begins. Their arrival as hungry, needy shoppers at six or seven can be a damaging thing in family life. *I need more credit.* Want renamed as need is sharp in the digital realm. Part of this wanting is about how we want to see ourselves. This can easily be in terms of the social gap between what others have and what we have. The digital realm is always upgrading its most highly desirable objects – phones, for example – and we are left behind if we don't add, upgrade, enhance or increase.

This isn't a rant against capitalism. It is about the consequences for our children of one-dimensional capitalism (which operates in the single dimension of profitability). All children are vulnerable. And they cannot withstand the pressure from clever advertising and the social gap. Children pick up the rules and the prevailing motives fairly quickly but, still, they are always born innocent. Before they possess adult objectivity their innocence is a valuable strength.

Mum, I need to top up. Saying *no* to a young digital addict is, to the parent, like denying him food when he is hungry. The lack of credit is felt as instant starvation. This is not an exaggeration, I am afraid. This is why it becomes important, as in the real world, to teach the value of things as we grow up by setting clear limits, agreeing on responsibilities and consequences. The problem of 'unlimited everything' is that it makes it hard to know where the edges are and that resources are finite. Scarcity has been banished but at a cost. Unlimited digital everything like unlimited food is hardly conducive to self-discipline and a lean energetic body. The glut overflows in urban environments, surrounding children with commercially led sound and images. It's almost impossible to escape them.

Isn't this just the way of things? Isn't this a brave new world of diverse communication? If it is, we need to foster in our children the strength for inner self-dependence as an adult so that when they encounter it they will not be its puppet. The seeds for this are really sown in the first few years and not in lessons about it in class ten.

Ed and Ellie's diary...

We agreed a rule and now, two weeks in, we've mostly stuck by it, despite a few blips. No phones in the kitchen or dining room during mealtimes. We have rediscovered eating together. The TV is off, even the radio, even music! It was a bit awkward at first, even felt cheesy. The conversation felt a bit forced, the silences a bit weird. But now we are getting used to it. We pass food to each other; we talk about our day, even argue a bit. The kids hate it, but Jules said this morning that he thought he was liking it a bit more. It's made me realize I was starting to lose touch with my own daughter. This is family time now. Meals are a bit rushed and I can sense Jules hurrying to get back online. But it's becoming a precious half an hour for the three of us. I wonder how long it will last?

Nick's diary

Well, that was a lot tougher than I thought it would be. She rarely has a tantrum and that one lasted for three days. Taking her tablet away from her for a whole week. One of my friends said it was cruel and unnecessary. We filled the week with some great activities. A trip down to the beach, the working farm and play area, plenty of outdoor stuff. She refused on the first day. When we got home there was a lot of screaming and I thought: Sheesh, she's actually an addict. Bella said we were lucky that we were doing this when she was still young enough. It really did only take a week. She's pretty OK now. She still asks, still pushes. But now we've introduced the idea of 'screen time'. And it's when we are there, three times a week, for an hour. But the pressure is on now. What to fill our week with. That was the big realization. The computer was simply covering up for the fact we weren't being a proper family.

Try this: encounter instead of escape

The next time you and your child see an advertisement, or the next time your child shows you an advert and says, 'I so need this,' take a breath and don't immediately answer. Look at the advert with your child and talk about it. Identify the advertisement's tricks. See if the child can 'crack the riddle' and work out the agenda. What is the advertisement trying to get you to do? Merely naming the game keeps you ahead. The child may then revise her 'I need this' to something less. She may not. Either way, she is less likely to remain a devotee of the cult of dissatisfaction. This cult chips away at innocence. If we, as parents, value that innocence we'll prevent the problem in the first place by controlling access to digital content in an age-appropriate way. Opening a dialogue with your children about the meanings of advertising images can be fun and creative and can lead to some shared areas of understanding and humour.

When children are entirely immersed in the digital realm, they forget the difference between want and need. Result: wanting eats away at the vitals. When *ordinary wanting* becomes *need*, something valuable in us is being switched off.

Try this: exploring need and want

Explore the difference between want and need. Share examples of real need in the world: hunger and famine, someone in need of a life-saving operation, people without a roof over their heads. You might look at some pictures together in a book or online. Or watch a film. Need is deep, often life or death.

We can acknowledge a child's strong sense of want, but helping him recognize what need really looks like helps him to make an important distinction. It restrains wanting which holds out for unrealistic dreams to make space for the serious sense of wanting, as in study, career and personal development. This fosters the realization that we have a life without all of our wants being fulfilled.

Wanting something for another, really and truly, is a beautiful human motive. If wanting and getting for oneself becomes the default setting at a young age it makes children cold, clever and manipulative. When this occurs it replaces wanting something for others with calculating self-interest. The child really can learn that our wants fit into a wider picture of human wants and that making the effort comes before real satisfaction. Toddlers are too young to be constantly wanting and getting, and their powerful will needs to be guided by the parent. The child who learns to love the protective guiding authority of the parent will eventually develop self-control and see the wider picture. It will develop the habit of wanting not as a single self alone but as a member of a family, a community and the world at large. And most likely, one day, as a selfless parent.

Over the course of researching this book, I've formed the view that the corporate commercial aspect of the digital realm attempts to fuse want and need together. We really need that new smartphone, we have to have a faster laptop. But do we, really? Really? Knowing your real needs actually strengthens your ability to make free decisions in the world. And it helps you concentrate, simply because wanting is just never ending. When the habit of dissatisfaction is established, children become whining, grasping, urgent and desperate, which are all symptoms of anguish.

So, there are different views and opinions.

At one end of the spectrum there is the libertarian approach. Children are going to get access to this stuff anyway; the digital realm will figure hugely in their lives and we might as well let them at it straight away. This is akin to putting the child out into the woods alone to shock it into growing up.

There is the indulgent approach. A significant and growing minority of under-fives in the UK now have mobile phones and tablet computers, which can now be bought styled in pink or blue with bouncy drop-proof covers. Many parents simply let their kids play online because they see it as no different to being up after the nine o'clock TV watershed. Life is tough, life is real and *hey, it didn't do me any harm*. So they say. (When parents have different views on what amount of protection and access is good for children then a real demand is put upon their communication and negotiation skills. Most kids need a good example and firm boundaries in order to acquire self-discipline and will be drawn to the cool parent who indulges them with treats. The one who wants to guide will be the nay-saying spoiler.)

A bit further along we have the parents who are not as laissez-faire but who still subscribe to the pro-digital view. The digital world is a training ground for learning and life. Tablets have dedicated apps for learning numbers, creative play, art, finding things out, stories and even for lessons in morality. As with the TV, tablet time can be a tempting child minder and proper filtering can keep the kids safe. Clearly, here, the parenting challenge is to stick to the right limits and keep the children safe. This will mean making conscious and well-informed choices as to what technologies they have access to and what applications are suitable for them. Careful parents always sit with their children during digital time. Others let them range freely within varying limits on time and access. The more libertarian parents will tend to set their kids loose with access to films and games that are above their recommended age. This is very dangerous as even Parental Guidance and 12 Certificate films can be very sexualized, violent and morally dubious.

Then further along again we have reactive parents who are sometimes confused. They often crumble in the face of arguments with their more savvy kids who benchmark themselves against their friends. If they attempt to use parental controls on their computers the kids work out how to get round them. They limit screen time with varying success, but often aren't good role models themselves.

The digital battleground is often a symptom of a weakening solidarity within the family.

Finally, there is that group of parents who believe that the digital inferno is not a place for children to wander in alone. They need to be introduced to it when the time is right. It can be different for different children, but over ten is a fair indication. They need to learn how it works, and they need to be kept safe. Such parents lead by example by consistently 'placing' their own digital activities in time and place. There might be a movie once or twice a week, which everyone watches together with some nice food. Films can provide a background of common reference and be a bond between family members rather than driving them apart into separate worlds.

When we make the home a place that kids like to be in there is no need for them to disengage. Parents can engage their children in activities that develop tastes and abilities which render digital attractions less tempting. At a recent camping festival I spoke to several parents who had brought their kids. They noticed that the ipads hadn't been asked for once, probably because there were plenty of other children there, as well as things for them to do.

A craving for digital distraction is often a sign that the parents are being poor role models. Parenting consumes time and energy. We need to play with our children, talk to them and give them plenty to do. The cry of 'there is nothing to do' is the symptom of the play impulse gone dead. We forget, at our peril, the benefits of family walks and sharing our wonder at the seasonal changes happening all around us. There are local sports, playgrounds, trips to local events, crafts, art, a treasure trove of stories and the sheer pleasure of one-on-one time with the children. When this family culture goes then screen time is the all too compelling option.

We can only really lead by example. It breeds trust. And we must be neither digital dinosaurs nor addicts. We need to lead the way and be able to understand the digital realm and speak its basic language. Parents can and, I think, should become better informed by becoming smarter inhabitants of the digital realm themselves, perhaps by going to a few classes. There is an opportunity here for parents to build bridges with their children. They could ask their children to share some emoticons or games or sites which they think are good. Showing an interest and asking some questions out of that interest will build common ground. The next time you message your child you might use one or two of the emoticons. Starting to speak their language, even a little, builds bridges by acknowledging their current world.

If we want to educate our kids to be safe, we must keep a dialogue going and reward their trustworthiness with trust in them. We can respect their teenage space as they can learn to respect our need for reassurance that they are safe and following agreed ground rules. As kids grow older, achieving the balance between real life and digital life needs to be the shared responsibility of all family members. If we want to stay in there, we parents need to be open to the way the world is evolving in general and have a warm interest in what our kids are doing, rather than defaulting to mistrust and policing.

One of our best resources for managing the digital challenge in family life is family life itself. Children need to grow up in families whose eating, sleeping and waking up times follow a rhythm, and in which the thoughts, feelings and tastes of the parents quietly express what they themselves look up to in life. All this will fit them for success, however you define it, far better than educational hothousing and being out working all hours to pay for the high status school. They'll take their digital trips away from us – even long ones which you may not learn about for years – but they'll be safe in their hearts and they will want to come back to us. They'll also confide in us if they are in trouble, and trouble can appear out of nowhere. They can get confused or worried, or be cyber-bullied. It will not serve to protect them if they keep their troubles to themselves because we snatched their devices away with an 'I told you so'.

Ellie's diary...

Yesterday Nick did something unprecedented. He stayed in on a Friday evening. He always goes out on a Friday evening. We agree a time for him to be home and then we spend Saturday arguing about why he came home later. It is usually a standing row in his bedroom and I've started to give way; it was just getting too tiring. And then this happened. I'd been up to London and visited Borough Market and came back via the Craft Fair. I was loaded with goodies. I bought a DVD as well for me and Stu to watch, and not a cheap one for once, something top ten. I made this Thai curry with all kinds of dips and a Caramel Apple Granny for dessert. I lit the candles and this really spicy, warming incense. And then Nick wandered in, sat down with us and I offered him some of the curry. He sniffed at it, ate it, had a glass of organic pinot, and watched the film. Neither me nor Stu said a word. Then afterwards we talked about the film and Nick told us about an argument he'd had with a teacher at school; it kind of related to the film. The dessert was perfectly timed and, before we all knew it, it was midnight. Nick yawned, wished us good night and headed off to his room. First time in years. I talked about it with Stu afterwards and he said: It isn't about stopping them going out. It's about making home a good reason to stay in.

Our own son is nine and is aware of this realm that runs parallel to the real one. We have a film night once a week but no TV. We love the fact that when we read him stories he makes his own inner pictures. We can almost see him doing it. And when the time is right he will slide into that realm armed and ready for action. As he becomes more aware and assertive we have to 'place' our devices more consciously. They have no place upstairs or at mealtimes. Stories, whether made up or from books, are magical and sweet and have inspiring heroes. There is a lot of talking and sometimes we include him in our conversations about digital things. He trusts us to shepherd him towards the digital realm in the right way and at the right time.

The family that heads out together into the world within walking distance of the home (sure, not always easy or even possible) starts having conversations about things which they have seen or done together. All of this can positively replace the need for everyone to head off to their rooms to find connection. Getting out and about to socialize is energizing and soon we forget we aren't online. One way of helping those kids who are too glued to their devices for us to risk the battle of removing them is to render them less relevant. I know that isn't easy, but it's the challenge for all parents: to create a home life that our kids don't want to get away from.

Ellie's diary...

We have parental controls set on our broadband connection. It's a pain really because it blocks a lot more than porn and gets in the way of my work. But we don't regret it. It keeps the kids safer. It surprised me to hear that not all broadband providers have controls as good as on ours. It seems as if they are playing catch-up. But you can't let them get onto a search engine with some of the images that come up. Of course, it doesn't stop what the kids might see at other houses. In the end, they will find their way into the darker side of our world, but at least we can try to do what we can to protect them until they are ready to make their own choices. But yesterday, we were all watching the news and suddenly there's this psychologist describing abuse in graphic details and I notice our youngest looking fascinated and a bit disturbed. Then, a few minutes later there's some film of a dog and its owner being washed down a river in a flood. And suddenly I am seeing that through my child's eyes and thinking, there's no way a child should be seeing that at nine. I sat her down and talked about what she'd seen. I told her the owner and her dog had probably been rescued and that the people who did bad things to other people were caught and locked away in prison. But those images are in there now, in her head, all mixed up with Harry Potter and Barbie. And I'm realizing, you can't rely on parental controls on a computer. Real parental control has to be a real parent.

Ed's diary . . .

The good thing about calling it 'screen time' is that you can then put a number on it. Screen time – three hours a week. And screen time can be used to cover both TV and computer time. Also I learned one big lesson from Jean. It isn't about restricting screen time; it's about seeing it as a positive choice. You can have three hours screen time per week. Kids of course compare that to their friends and ours complain that their 'screen time' is less than what their friends get. Kids will always compare to their friends and then it is back to saying they are being held back again. So we tried a week with no screen time. The kids kicked up one hell of a stink but we stuck with it. We went on a few trips and out for a really nice meal. We went to the theatre as well. Then we went into the next week with a clear rule: three hours' screen time. In relation to no screen time, it feels like plenty to them at the moment. And if they break the rule, then they know it's going to be a week of no screen time.

Sarah's diary . . .

It's working. The deal is simple. They get an hour extra screen time for every hour we all walk together. It's primitive but it is working. On Saturday afternoon, they get to play on their devices for two hours and then, at four, we all go for a walk on the Downs, whatever the weather. It's beautiful up there. Sometimes we all talk, sometimes the kids moan, but at least they are getting exercise. Saturday last we actually got into a conversation about the game they all seem to be addicted to that involves building an entire city and putting people in it, houses, even deciding on the culture of this virtual world! Mel tried to explain it to us and we both asked a lot of questions. In fact, we talked for over an hour, and now I've noticed Mel talks to me more about what she is doing on the computer. I don't always get what she is trying to explain but I give her a good listen. Now the walking deal has become routine and both Mel and Ed have got more colour in their cheeks. I always take a snack with us and, if it's raining, we stop at Carlo's on the way back for a treat.

Roe's diary...

When Dean gets home he is straight upstairs. The door slams and he's in his virtual world. He comes down to supper reluctantly and pushes for eating in his room. In some ways I'm glad he's at home rather than up to mischief on the streets somewhere, but we don't see much of him these days. He's 14 and there's not much we can do. Stopping him using the computer will just alienate him further. We've tried everything. What really worries me is who he might be talking to up there. It could be anyone. He tells me not to worry, but when I asked if I could sit with him for a bit while he's 'chatting' he told me, 'No way.' I actually joked to Maria that, 'It's like he's already left home even though he is still physically in the house.' She nodded and made some suggestions. 'You all need to go to a music festival. Or send him Inter-railing.' Actually we'd said no to him going to a music festival, and an even bigger 'no' to going to Amsterdam with his mates. Maria offered to lend me one of her tents. Tents? We haven't been camping in years! 'He needs a life that is better than the one in his bedroom,' Maria said. She's right about that. Yesterday I was chatting to his friend's mum, Anita. She'd said her son was asking for permission to go Inter-railing this summer. You get a train ticket that takes you anywhere for two weeks. Anita asked what I thought of the idea. Weren't they too young? Then this morning I happened to go into Dean's room with some clean washing. He'd left his PC on. The image on the screen made me drop the washing. And Maria's words came right back to me: 'He needs a life that is better than the one in his bedroom...'

A lot of this advice might seem old-fashioned and out of touch with the realities of modern children and families. I don't believe it is out of date. I humbly suggest that it is absolutely timeless and only seems old hat because we have forgotten a lot of it. If the tender experiences of childhood which make a child into a strong adult are replaced by experiences which are child-unfriendly then the poor child doesn't develop in the best way. This can leave him at odds with himself, antisocial and under-achieving. At that point we start to preach ideas to him. Then when that does not work, and if he begins to seriously fail in life, he will probably end up being punished by life and possibly by the law. Brilliant! The making of a person starts way back and the digital realm does not help it to get off to the right start.

Family time, connection to nature, physical exercise and shared activities are some foundation stones for growing up confident, curious and feeling safe and held. All of that might sound too uncool. I think it is not about cool. Cool is just about fashions. This real stuff is about timeless principles:

- *showing an interest in what children are doing*
- *showing leadership and authority as a parent and setting limits that keep them safe*
- *linking access to screens to good habits, so screen time is allowed after kids meet parents halfway by eating well and being active*
- *doing things together as a family to meet the communication needs that the child otherwise seeks online*
- *being able to speak their language and see them as a source of savvy 'know how' about the digital realm*

I believe that in the child's early years the balance between the real and the digital worlds should be struck at a ratio of one hundred per cent to zero in favour of the real, three-dimensional world. Let children be children. Let them run around and give their bodies the space to do what they have to do. Protect them from high intensity artificial stimulation so their immature nervous systems have the peace to do what they have to do. Let them make their own inner pictures. These will come out if we do not stuff others in there first. Wait. Wait until they are really ready and prime your intuition so it tells you when that is.

Playfulness and innocence in children often stir something sentimental in the heart of a parent, but sometimes the parent still can't join the dots and still addresses the child as a little grown-up. 'Do you want to stay out, or shall we go home?' The toddler is perplexed the first few times but if we continue to address it as a little grown-up, he or she will step into that role quickly. And children can quickly *appear* to be little adults. But the child feels safe and held when the parent surrounds it with loving authority. Then the child feels that it can leave the detail to mum and dad and turn its curiosity to the interesting things going on all around it. It does not have to work up a frown for making its next so-called choice.

Anxiety, depression and lack of confidence in later life are increasingly being traced back to the overloading of children in their early years with stress and high stimulation. Common sense fuses with science here. The brain of the child in the first few years is like a new house after the wiring's put in but not connected up. The connecting up can happen well or not well and how well it turns out is the direct result of everything that happens to the child and around it. Truly, the importance of this matter is hard to overestimate.

But back to all-important play — play is an ongoing creating of something. Being free to unfold in childhood play instils *faith in our ability to move forward with the confidence to invent responses as we go.* (This strength can still work deeply in us as adults, to help us fulfil our potential and face challenges.) Play preserves the child's self-confidence. All of that exploration becomes confidence for learning in the lower school. When the child is ready for formal teaching and it is right for him to focus in a new way, digital technology will be one of the subject areas. But it's more helpful at eleven than at three. At three, anything which children play with should work in such a way that they can understand it, such as a real balancing scale or a real grinding stone, a real paintbrush instead of a painting app. The reason is that it is possible for the child's understanding to 'reach into' such things. This is not possible with any electrical device. Buckets of water and a big sandpit are far more educational for the young child than an app and a screen.

Is this old-fashioned? If it is, then maybe it is old-fashioned like lots of other things which have been around for ages – for the simple reason that they are archetypal and are part of our nature.

There's no easy way round this. Parenting kids with screen time isn't funky. It's flaky.

A checklist for parenting in the digital inferno

1. Have a conversation with your child about safety in the digital realm. Ensure they don't feel criticized. Find out what they know about safety. Let them know the door is open and that you won't be judging them or punishing them. Let them know that you want them to be safe and that it is your prime concern. If you can, get them to show you how they practise being safe in the digital realm.

2. Set up some rhythms around screen time which preserves family time in the right way. Link screen time to physical exercise and outdoor activities.

3. 'Place' screen time in time and place. Get devices out of the kitchen, especially during mealtimes. Preferably, create a space for using devices. Have agreed family time when no one in the family is *on*.

4. *For younger children, always be present with them when they are on devices, or watching films or TV.* Do it with them. Talk to them about what they are seeing. Tune in to their tastes and their sense of humour. Don't use the device as a child minder.

5. Engage your younger children in creative activities away from

screens so they can create their own images with imaginative games, dressing up and play acting, drawing, painting and storytelling. There is often storytelling in local libraries, but kids really love the home-made ones. They don't have to be masterpieces.

6. Take them to places where digital devices are irrelevant because the real world is so fresh and alive. Camping is the best example, or swimming or rock-pooling by the sea. In cities, find galleries, museums, local parks and playgrounds. Expose the child to nature and the arts. The young child who sees how you value different kinds of beauty will learn to do the same. Hobbies such as cooking and growing or collecting things can all help. Interesting relatives – such as wise grandparents full of stories – are also part of your armoury of alternatives to screen time.

7. Set limits on screen time. Overcome initial resistance, stick to your guns and link screen time to certain family treats. Keep screen time away from preparing for sleep, getting ready for school and mealtimes. *Do this positively* as in 'this is when screen time is' rather than 'this is when you can't have it'.

8. Acknowledge their interest in the digital realm. Be clued up enough to talk about it and ensure they know the basics of how the devices work. Buy a book, take a trip to the library, attend a workshop together. Don't be a fuddy-duddy.

9. Dive in together. Ensure screen time is shared time. Go online together, either in the same room or different rooms, with the rule being that you then come back together. Share what you've been doing. Share experiences, questions, dilemmas, and worries. Reduce the likelihood that your children will want to be online furtively, away from you.

10. Show an interest in the arts, social trends, developing issues and world affairs. Maintain shared interests in the real world. Read out part of a news story that might be of interest to everyone in the family. *Viral stories*, the ones that have spread

quickly in the digital realm, can generate beliefs and opinions deserving of some careful discussion. 'Hyper-local news' (local news at street level) can be a way of engaging in our immediate communities. It is generated by local TV and radio stations, but is now also to be found in social media status updates and tweets. 'Did you hear? ... there's a free outdoor concert in the park tonight ... George, at number 42, just said he saw some kind of snake in his front garden.'

11. Recognize perhaps that your role, especially with teenagers immersed in the digital realm, is not going to be to attempt to snatch back traditional parenting based on authority and control. In some cases, especially where your son or daughter is very clued up, immersed and 'happy' being a digital native, you might do better as a critical friend, a collaborator and to acknowledge their activity, become a bit clued up yourself so you can talk their language and not appear alienated from their lives. Alongside trying to offer attractive alternatives to nearly constant digital immersion this can give your alternatives the credibility that is needed for the youngsters to voluntarily limit their screen time.

12. Lead by example. What kind of example are you currently setting to your kids? Are you the 'digiholic' who commands your kids to 'do as I say not as I do'? Practise many of the activities offered in this book, create some conscious placement and balance yourself. If you use it, but don't abuse it, you might just find that leading by example rubs off on your children and you don't have to tell them anything at all about the good and bad aspects. Or they might just come and ask.

16

Welcome to the Internet of Things — the Future

A device in your house registers what time you are coming home because another device in your car sends a message to it, and the heating is activated, so that you enter a warm house. You look at certain clothes in a store and your actions are recorded on a database which collates all your consumer interests and you receive special offers by email targeted to your tastes. Your watch is keeping tabs on your heart rate and the data is available to your doctor for your next check-up. A bedside lamp is programmed to measure your sleeping child's vital signs, alerting you to changes in their breathing or perhaps to some bad dream they might be having. This is the internet of things, the next phase of the digital inferno's development. It has already begun.

Embedding of internet-enabled devices into more and more of our environment will set homes, schools, public buildings, social spaces and places of work to an always-on state. It is benevolent where there is a useful service to humankind but sinister when we are being spied on, manipulated and covertly controlled. There will be digital 'conversations' about us invisibly zig-zagging around us. Yes, it points to a massive step in the service of humanity by digital technology, or to a massive step in the subversion of human goals by corporations and governments, or to both these steps at the same time. The internet of things is influencing how we interact with each other and with our physical and digital environments. Doors may slam in our faces, rooms will adjust their temperature, producers and service providers will try to gain our purchasing attention, and hyper-distraction may eclipse the calm and sacred thoughts we still cling to.

The internet of things will require us to be mindful and conscious. Placement is going to be more difficult if we are always on. In making clear choices about what technology we buy we should take into account how much real freedom we have to switch them off and to control the settings. Of course, I have stated elsewhere in this book that you might decide to accept the invitation to surrender, to dive in and let the internet of things function merrily around you and possibly even inside you. If you aren't ready or willing to surrender quite yet, then the internet of things is going to (and is already beginning to) surround you, enfold you, and begin to shape your day.

We already are being watched by security cameras. Our behaviour is being tracked by the devices we use and processed into information and then into various kinds of product offers. In the past, 'intelligent' technology amounted to the safety cut-out on our gas cooker. In the emerging future, these things will connect up and form part of a larger system. The self-driving, self-navigating car, the cooker that learns and adapts to your cooking style, the sleeping shades that also influence what you dream . . .

At home we'll be seeing three things increasingly connecting up, between and across them: home security, automation of home devices (lighting, heating, cooking) and home entertainment. They'll be based on a new operating system, a bit like the operating system for your computer or smartphone which is written especially for connecting things up and enabling them to mesh their functions.

So, the digital realm will incarnate into the very things we pick up and use in our physical lives. That's the new frontier in the digital realm. And already hot on its heels is the internet of 'us', the emergence of the digital in the physical body of the human being. It's been shaping our brains and the way we think for decades – it's been influencing our soul life, largely without our notice (hence the need for books like this one), and advanced steps are already being made towards the creation of the cyborg, the machine-in-the-human, the bionic arm, the electronically stimulated brain, the enhancement of our senses from Google Glasses to digitally assisted physical eyes.

There could be many benefits. But without knowing its impact, it could bring as much darkness as light. We already know that digital connectedness links us to the corporation; in that partnership we are by far the weaklings. We also know that digital distraction and addiction is not at all good. We are aware that our originality and creativity can be compromised by constant exposure to repetition and cliché. A whole culture is becoming monopolized by a series of pre-set associations and narrowed meanings by the power of digital images. The internet of things is coming so very rapidly and it is riding a wave of innovation that is flowing much faster than any social or medical research. We are exposed to covert dangers when change runs faster than our ability to learn and reflect. They will compromise our freedom, especially the freedom of those who are not able to stand up to it. One of the dangers posed by the internet of things (and the interests behind it) will be its power to define who and what we are, what we see and feel, how we see and feel it, and what our own next steps should be. When the physical things around us, the things we touch and use, are wired in together in a way that is impossible for us to detect, understand or control then we had better make damn sure we can trust whatever electronic transactions are occurring between them.

I'm not against the internet of things. I am sounding a warning. Our kids will grow into these things naturally. They'll grow into a world where the lights adjust themselves to the perfect level. They'll also grow into a world where a physical door may slam in their face because they haven't paid a credit card bill. Shops will increasingly know who they are and what they like by what they look at and pick up. There's a real danger that we become even more passive, that we default to the 'smart' decisions offered by the devices. There's a danger that, even as we benefit in one way, our will forces for making the critical decisions in our life will become weaker. There's a danger that the internet of things will also label us, simplify us and in the name of efficiency encourage us to take the shortest but not always the most spiritually nourishing or beautiful route.

The internet of things may well evolve into something incredible and wonderful. If the way the digital realm has evolved so far is anything to go by, it will be clunky to start with but it will be talked up by the press and enthusiasts of all stripes and their advocacy of it will be one-sided. It will shove rather than nudge. We'd do well to stay awake so we can choose the steps that we really want to take. Letting it happen around us without becoming informed will be bad for us.

Try this: an internet of things audit

On your next journey into work, into town, to school, from the moment you get up to the moment you get home, pay attention to the things that are in communication with each other, that in some way affect you. Pay attention also to the technologies that react in some way to you. For example:

- the motion sensors that become activated when you switch on the burglar alarm on your way out
- the automated ticket machine on the bus or train that takes some of your credit
- the automatic door that opens for you as you enter a shop
- the car seat belt alert that won't let you drive until you belt up
- the light that automatically switches on in the public toilet

Also pay attention to those things that are talking to other things:

- the security camera that is relaying to a bank of screens hidden somewhere
- the little payment machine in the restaurant that can identify who you are and where you live
- the sensors attached to a traffic light that record data in order to see if the lights need retiming
- the smartphone that tells you where you are and plots your quickest route to somewhere

---

Taking moments to simply be attentive to what is going on around us will be necessary for staying awake in this new world. It will become even more important when digital sensors, controls and displays are embedded in ordinary physical objects. It will not help to be clueless. If I know that my shopping behaviour is going to be tracked and measured in order to then target me with personalized advertising when I next switch on the TV or computer, I might decide not to enter that shop. An uninformed relationship to the internet of things is going to blow my privacy out of the water. A dark view of the future? If you've recently bought anything online, you'll find it's already happening. Looking at a website for some sun cream will have you targeted with adverts for late bookings to holiday destinations. Buying a memorial wreath online will soon have you targeted with offers for funeral services and life insurance policies.

What we'll gain will save lives and it will ensure that our technologies join up more effectively. *What we'll lose are spaces that are truly digitally empty.* We will lose the ability to unhitch from the digital realm. Staying awake will require us to be more attentive to the digital realm of things so that we have some way of ensuring that the freedom and individuality we seek in the centre of our lives is not compromised.

Try this: Imagining your way into the digital thing

This is a little imagination exercise. It helps you keep your 'imagination muscle' in good shape and allows you to practise staying alert in an encompassing digital realm. Choose a thing that uses digital technology. For example, your smartphone, or a security camera. You could also choose a burglar alarm linked to the local police station, a credit card payment machine in a shop, a cash till, or a self-service check-in desk at an airport. You can run this imagination silently, in your head, or you could write everything down. Now, imagine as many of the digital processes that are taking place back along the line from the digital thing in front of you. Imagine how the digital thing might be connecting or communicating with other digital devices which are not in front of you.

For example: your smartphone alerts you to a message.

The message has come from someone else's smartphone.

The person, when typing it, was somewhere which could have been more or less private.

The message has lit up on your phone, and you are in more or less of a private place yourself.

The message was delivered digitally so it was sent via a third party.

The message is stored somewhere now, on the sender's phone, on yours, and probably at least in one other place.

Keywords in the message have been analysed, possibly by security services, and at least in order to target you with products and services related to the keywords.

The message has been copied to someone else who may or may not read it, respond to it, act on it or store it.

The fact that you have read a text has been recorded on your phone and by the service provider.

If you've read a lot of messages and reply a lot, this has been recorded and noted in a database. The message is being observed as part of a bigger analytical picture of your messaging behaviour.

And so on...

Observe as many things as you can about the digital thing and its interaction with you, your surroundings and other digital things. Doing this might prompt you to do some research in order to gain a better understanding of how digital processes actually work. One thing you will discover (and may have already discovered to your annoyance or surprise) is your own unintended yet seemingly undeletable imprint. Your quick search for a book online results in being targeted with all kinds of more or less related adverts. Amid all the noise and the swirl, a key priority for corporations and those attempting to govern the digital realm is identifying you as a target. 'Personalization', as it is often called, in order to improve your 'user experience', is all about targeting you.

The digital inferno is wrapping itself around and inside the very physical things we use. We may even breathe the digital in through nano-robots smaller than a flea's eye. One will find out why we have a pain in a kidney. Another might infect us as part of a chemical weapon. As with anything new, exciting and potentially dangerous, it is better to be awake, clued up and ready than to surrender to something we might just regret later on.

17

Going Back Consciously into the Digital Realm – Enjoying the Dance

The purpose of this book was to offer one traveller's guide to the digital realm. I've called it an inferno because of its seething nature which can drag us down and burn us. In there, we can lose ourselves to distraction, addiction, confusion, exploitation and worse.

The digital realm offers us control, entertainment and information that have never been available before. It offers ease and escape into simulated, virtual worlds to rival some of our wildest dreams. It is beginning to offer extensions of our sense organs. It offers instant publishing to the world. It lets us work from anywhere, find our way in strange cities and see just about any building in the world. It can pinpoint where we are on earth and identify the stars, show the weather in real time and bring moving images of family members from thousands of miles away into our home. It can offer us access to the world's libraries, archives, books, films, music and works of art. We can broadcast over it, find love, or at least a date, and order just about anything, from hot food to helicopters. We can even leave a recording of our beating heart in a digital mausoleum. It represents the genius of human invention and slowly but surely it is giving birth to digital entities that are remaking it from within. It is creating a connected world community that enables both peacemakers and terrorists to connect up. We can dive in day and night and find stimulation and affirmation there. We can create second lives which we prioritize over our real life. It can enable the sharing of learning, insight and expertise. It can create wealth. It can become a place to share passionate ideas and feelings. It can link people and communities, allow individuals to explore and share differences, and it can be a base from which to develop personally and professionally. It is the meeting point for different motives — from pure, unregulated greed to benevolent attempts to empower and enable.

We can become its plaything while believing we are in control. We may feel we dived in too deeply and too quickly, or we may feel we are skimming its surface and not getting value from it. We might want to immerse ourselves and experience it without limit. Some are doing that and there are no *long-term* studies on the effects. Some studies and stories advise caution and this book attempts to offer perspectives on that. I've suggested that you will experience it in the best way if you strengthen your will to meet its 'pull' with inner strength – I mean the kind of strength which gives you a good idea of what your life is about in the real world.

Most of the digital realm's shadowy places are a fait accompli. But, enthusiasts say, it is actually a fairly harmless realm and it is necessary to dive into it in case you are left behind. To have misgivings about some of the other partygoers is just being down on the fun, they say. But the idea that the digital realm is a party that we'd be crazy not to show up to is just false. The choice lies with each person, needless to say, to place the digital realm, with *more* or *less* awareness of the full picture, in his or her life. I have presented a harsh view of the digital realm in some parts of this book. I wonder at anyone who denies that the changes wrought by it, in personal and economic life as well as in wider culture, have received insufficient consideration. And even our spiritual life. Like a giant octopus it envelops the world and it is hard for anyone to get an overview. The digital realm needs to be scrutinized not only by statistical science but also by individuals with common sense. It just does. I wonder at those who do not see this. The safety and sanity of too many, both young and old, are at stake. We need not simply 'submit'.

Writing this book grew out of my view that it was time to question our faith in the digital realm. My starting point was that many people over the years, whom I have observed at first hand, are suffering in it through losing aspects of themselves, as well their friends and families. I was shocked at how 'unsavvy' people could be in their dealings with it while being, in other parts of their lives, perfectly on the case. It was obvious to me that invaluable aspects of the culture of childhood were being lost, and that even small children were being drawn into games that instilled a hunger which only grew by trying to satisfy it.

OK, here's this thing, I thought to myself, as big as a new world, a paradigm shift as profound as any that has ever taken place: the digital revolution. Its spiderlike web-nature tries to draw us into its centre. That image helps to focus the mind on the need to protect ourselves. But I also thought it necessary to ask myself how to get the best of it.

This required engaging with its different faces. There is a battle over the nature of childhood and the effects of the digital realm on children in homes and schools. There is a new economic carve-up. There is even a battle for the image we collectively hold up to ourselves of what a human being is and will become. There is the prospect of a powerful, flexible servant directed by its human masters as a means to free human ends. There is the prospect of an alien nature emerging under our noses.

What's this nonsense about an alien thing? I'm not crazy. It is a useful way to look at the future of the digital realm. The emerging notion of 'Big Data' is throwing up new forms of computing that go way beyond what human beings are capable of, even what most current computers are capable of. With more complex data storage and lightning fast processing speeds we can make calculations and analyses that lie way, way beyond the human brain's capacity. We are creating awesome digital entities, often working for months on end with only occasional human direction. We are interested in the processed output, the useful results while the programs themselves run in ways that go beyond normal human thinking. The hyper-computers of the near future will feel alien to us. We ourselves will develop them but will not fully understand the outcomes. As we attempt to get closer to unlocking the secrets of nature, the quantum computers will partly 'invent' ways of ordering complex data sets. Humans will do some input, to an extent, and get some output, but in terms of the core processes in the digital realm, they'll get the hell out of the way. This was envisioned by science fiction. The Rise of the Machines. Our android-like picture of them is quaint. The digital entities of the future will not look like us but may emerge as another form. For example, an increasing proportion of the digital inferno operates with minimal human intervention. The extent to which that will become boon or bane in the long term is unknown. The seeds are already planted in the realm of automation. Many processes of buying online now involve little or no human involvement at all until the product is on the truck for delivery and even delivery may soon be by robotic drones, flying their way to our doorsteps. It is already in the pilot stage.

Last thoughts

A good approach to the inferno will be to consider how we tend to have one-sided views on things. There is one extreme of letting ourselves go — *let's not think about it too much, let it overwhelm us* — and another, of fixing on some view, and both are ways of losing oneself. Between these is a way of finding ourselves that does not derive from or fix on any single idea, or on ideas at all. It is a mobile and alive way of finding ourselves through thinking and feeling in action. Another way of pointing to what I mean is by calling attention to the experience we can have of an active, inner self — even though this is something which never can be pointed to because each one of us only grasps the self *alone*, as we are making it happen. This mobile way of finding ourselves is a concern running through this book, that in the new digital world it must be *we* who choose the dance we move to.

The dance can become truly our own when it is not merely a matter of making a choice between predispositions. When these, as underlying motives for our actions, are transparent to us then we are not merely unconsciously determined. Then our imagination can create a motive the driving force for which is none other than our own self. This book has been written to encourage readers to deal with the digital realm from the standpoint of their own freedom. We can tear free of its entwining arms. The gadget only serves us when we engage from a position of independence. We are not gadgets but beings who are potentially the first cause of our actions, that is, potentially undetermined or free. The addictive pull is indeed a threat to our freedom and to much else. But if we place the digital realm in our homes and daily lives with a purpose which we love because it is a good purpose, then we have a chance of engaging with it as free individuals. First we must know ourselves.

It may be that your time has come to reclaim your self from the digital inferno – to step back, to reflect and to restore some of your stolen will-power. You may have to detoxify, admit your addiction, work on reducing the pull and becoming more conscious of the digital inferno. You may realize how your thoughts translate into the steps you take in the digital realm, and that the weaker your will the more easily you'll 'submit' and be subject to its chaos. You can move from being an addict to being a mindful master in the digital realm when you direct your self with will, stepping eloquently beyond the reach of the dead spiderlike arms with a living dance of your own.

Bibliography

There are numerous books and studies on the digital realm, though the total amount of definitive social research is fairly thin on the ground. Here I include some books and studies that might help you in your further research and which have helped to inform and inspire some of the contents of this book.

Adams, Gemini, *The Facebook Diet: 50 Funny Signs of Facebook Addiction and Ways to Unplug with a Digital Detox*, Adams, Live Consciously, 2013

Brockman, John (Editor), *How is the Internet Changing the Way You Think*, Atlantic Books, London 2012

Castells, Manuel, *Networks of Outrage and Hope: Social Movements in the Internet Age*, Polity Press, 2012

Hart, Archibald D., and Hart Frejd, Sylvia, *The Digital Invasion: How Technology Is Shaping You and Your Relationships*, Baker Books, 2013

Lanier, Jaron, *You are Not a Gadget: A Manifesto*, Penguin Books, 2011

Lievegoed, Bernard, *Towards the 21st Century*, SteinerBooks, 1989

Livingstone, Sonia, *Children and the Internet*, Polity, 2009

Marzougui, Sara, *Life Without It*, CreateSpace Independent Publishing Platform, 2012; Amazon Kindle, 2012

Palmer, Sue, *Toxic Childhood: How the Modern World is Damaging Our Children And What We Can Do About It*, Orion, 2007

Pont, Simon, *Digital State: How the Internet is Changing Everything*, Kogan Page, 2013

Schmidt, Eric, and Cohen, Jared, *The New Digital Age: Reshaping the Future of People, Nations and Business*, John Murray, 2013

Slouka, Mark, *War of the Worlds: Cyberspace and the High-tech Assault on Reality*, Basic Books, 1995

Schwartz, Eugene, various articles in *Millennial Child*, http://www.millennialchild.com/

Turkle, Sherry, *Alone Together*, Basic Books, 2011

Zuckerman, Ethan, *Rewire: Digital Cosmopolitans in the Age of Connection*, W.W. Norton & Co., 2013

Studies

There are many studies into the effects of mobile phones on human health, and a few that are referred to in this book are listed below. I examined over 100 conflicting studies. More are being published all the time. There is less research into the social consequences of the currently emerging digital inferno. It is almost as if academics are playing catch-up. The social and psychological consequences of the digital realm are yet to be thoroughly researched, though authors such as Sherry Turkle (listed above) have made a bold start.

European Commission Scientific Committee on Emerging and Newly Identified Health Risks (SCENIHR), 'Conclusions on mobile phones and radio frequency fields'. Retrieved 8 December 2008. http://ec.europa.eu/health/opinions2/en/electromagnetic-fields/l-3/5-conclusions-mobile-phones.htm)

Parker-Pope, Tara, 'Piercing the Fog Around Cellphones and Cancer', *New York Times*, 7 June 2011. http://well.blogs.nytimes.com/2011/06/06/piercing-the-fog-around-cellphones-and-cancer/?_r=0)

Sadetzki, Siegal; Chetrit, Angela; Jarus-Hakak, Avital; Cardis, Elisabeth, et al., 'Cellular phone use and risk of benign and malignant parotid gland tumors—A nationwide case-control study', *American Journal of Epidemiology* (2008), 167 (4): 457–467 first published online 6 December 2007 doi:10.1093/aje/kwm325)

Wargo, John, Professor of Risk Analysis and Environmental Policy at Yale University, author of 'Cell Phones: Technology, Exposures, Health Effects', *Environment and Human Health, Inc. Monograph* 7, inc www.ehhi.org, published in 2012 http://www.ehhi.org/reports/cellphones/cell_phone_report_EHHI_Feb2012.pdf

'IARC classifies radiofrequency electromagnetic fields as possibly carcinogenic to humans' (PDF), press release No 208 31 May 2011

Glossary

It is easy to be bamboozled in the digital inferno. Here are some brief descriptions of some of the terms used for discussing the digital realm.

App/application   A digital program; a game or something useful for work or play, usually located on smartphones and tablet computers.

Augmented reality   A digital technology that adds to or enhances our sense experience of the physical world. An example is a car satellite navigation system. Augmented reality aims to help us to see more, further, clearer and differently.

Avatar   A digital identity we can create for ourselves that is more or less a true or fictional version of ourselves — it can be used in social media and within digital gaming.

Big data   The phenomenon of and practices around managing huge amounts of data.

Blogging   The sharing of a diary in the digital world; also articles, photos and other media for others to see and comment upon.

Bluetooth   A proprietary technology that allows wireless connection of devices. For example, the ability to speak on the phone using a wireless microphone headset.

Chat   The process of typed, audio or video talking in the digital realm.

Chat room   A shared digital space for typed, audio or video conversation between more than one person.

Cyborg   A being that combines human and robotic technology; a joining of technology and human biology.

Digitizing/digitalization   The process of rendering something from the physical world into digital format.

Digital inferno   My term to describe the powerful and ever-changing swirl of digital things, people and processes.

Digital realm   This is a name for the 'space' we are in whenever we are doing anything digital.

Email   A digital message that can be sent to anyone in the digital realm with an email address.

Emoticon   Small icons and symbols that are used to express emotion in digital communication. The smiley is an example.

Facebook   The most popular social media platform where people can share content: photos, thoughts, videos, and to collaborate, chat and play games together. A 'timeline' is a historical record of that activity.

Followers   People who follow some aspect of your activity in the digital realm.

Inbox   A digital folder for incoming email.

Internet of things   Embeds digital connectivity and functionality into the things around us, the things in our hands, the things we wear on our bodies.

IPad   A popular form of tablet computer.

Iphone   One of the world's best-selling mobile/cell phones.

Like   The ability to vote positively for an action in the digital realm. For example, an update or a photo.

LinkedIn   A more business-focused social media platform.

LOL   A form of digital 'text speak' which stands for a digital version of a physical response, in this case 'laugh out loud'.

Microblogging   The general term of sharing thoughts in small chunks — short sentences, images or short audio or video recordings.

Online   The state of being active in the digital inferno. You are 'online' when you are messaging but also when you are inactive but your computer is still connected to the internet.

Pixel   A dot on the screen — all digital pages are made up of pixels.

Pixelation   The process of turning a physical world image into a digital one.

Platform   The general term for a product or service people use in the digital realm. For example, Facebook.

Retweeting   The process of reposting a tweet to your followers.

Simulation   A programme in the digital realm that simulates something physical. For example, a flight simulator.

Social media   The general term for platforms which offer social interaction between people, groups and organizations.

Second life   The name of a popular virtual world website.

Skype One of the most popular audio calling methods in the digital realm.

Smiley A particular kind of emoticon that is usually a yellow smiling face.

SMS A text message.

Social media The various platforms and applications in the digital realm that allow individuals, groups and communities to interact with each other in social ways.

Tablet A portable form of computer.

Technosophy An approach to designing technological devices that users describe as 'wise' in their design. They are designed in very intelligent ways that respond to the real needs of those who use them.

Threaded discussion This is a typed or recorded comment usually posted by a person about an online bit of content, some text, a video or some music. People 'comment'. Threads grow when more comments are added by other people.

Tweet The word used to describe a post of 140 characters or less.

Twitter A platform enabling people to publish thoughts, links and images in 140 characters or less.

Vimeo A popular video-sharing platform, similar to YouTube.

Virtual reality A term used to describe a rendition of the physical world into the digital realm and also new forms of reality not inspired by the physical world.

Virtual world A simulated or imagined world in the digital realm, rendered in graphics and sound, often in three dimensions.

WILFing ('What was I looking for?') The process of being distracted by digital content, leading to moving away from one's original purpose or task. For example, you start with the intention of replying to an email. Whilst doing so you are distracted by an advert, click on the link and end up reading about holidays in Spain!

X The digital gesture for a physical kiss.

Yammer Another micro-blogging platform, like Twitter, popular with businesses and organizations.

YouTube A platform for sharing and commenting on video content.